Usborne Guide to MODEL AIRCRAFT

John Stroud

Designed by **Iain Ashman**   Edited by **Lynn Myring**

CONTENTS

2 Introducing model planes	14 Model engines	26 Odd models
4 How planes fly	16 Powered free-flight	28 Models at work
6 Building with balsa wood	18 Flying on control-lines	30 Plane words
8 First flights	20 Indoor flying	31 Going further
10 Model gliders	22 Radio-control	
12 Rubber-powered planes	24 Aerobatics and Racing	32 Index

Illustrated by
Basil Arm, Mike Baber, Terry Gabbey,
Mike Roffe, Swanston Associates,
Craig Warwick, Gordon Wylie.

INTRODUCING MODEL PLANES

When you begin building model planes you will find there are many types to choose from. Models are divided into groups according to the way in which they fly. The chart below explains the main groups and shows some of the aircraft to be found in them. If you are a learner pilot look for models referred to as "trainers". These are designed to be easy to make and to fly. Competition models are designed to fulfil the rules of a particular contest and sports models are ordinary non-contest planes.

Most models can be bought ready-made or you can build your own, either from kits or plans. Kits provide all the materials you need but with a plan you have to buy the materials separately.

Beginner's guide

If you have never made a model it is probably best to start with a kit. Look around the model shops for a glider or rubber-powered model made from sheet balsa wood. Choose something small and simple for a first model. It will teach you the basic skills needed to make and fly larger, more difficult models. Next, try a slightly larger

Gliders

Gliders are not powered in any way but are kept airborne by breezes and warm air currents. This means they have to be light in weight and have wings shaped to give lots of lift.
(See pages 10-11 for more about gliders.)

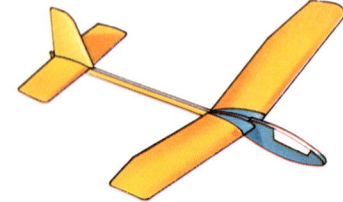

▲A sheet balsa wood "chuck" or hand-launched glider, is the simplest kind of model aircraft.

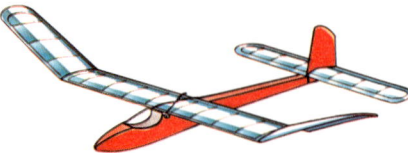

▲This "built-up" frame glider is made from strip balsa and covered in tissue. It is easy to make and fly.

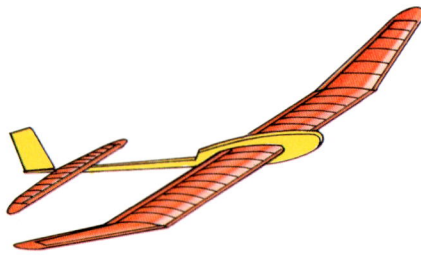

▲Competition gliders can be very large. Most have some automatic controls that are preset before take-off.

Rubber-powered

Rubber-powered models are propelled by the unwinding of strips of rubber, known as the motor. They are often similar in construction to gliders.
(See pages 12-13 for more about rubber-power.)

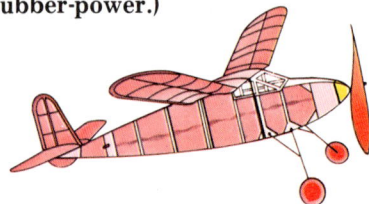

▲This is a typical sports model, with a built-up box fuselage and high wings to give stable flight.

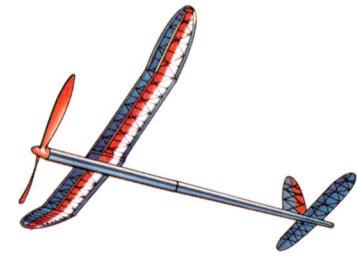

▲Competition models have to conform to contest rules. They are designed to fly for as long as possible.

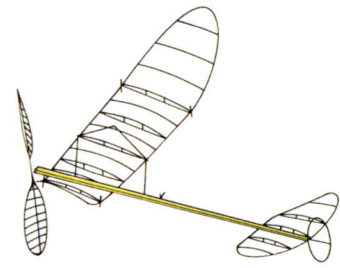

▲Indoor models are very light and fly extremely slowly. This kind of model is difficult to make and fly.

Engine-powered

Engine-powered models do not need to be as light as other free-flight models. The three most common kinds of miniature engines are explained on pages 14 and 15.
(See pages 16-17 for more about powered flight.)

▲This sports model is built from sheet balsa and needs only a small engine. This design flies very well.

▲Competition models are very sophisticated and have powerful engines that take them very high.

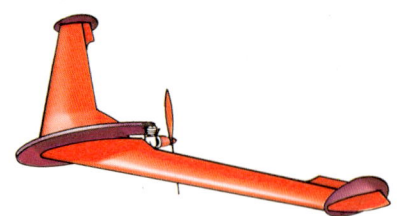

▲This is called a flying wing. The engine is at the back and it pushes the plane forwards.

glider or rubber-powered model, built up from strip balsa and covered with tissue paper.

▶The list on the right suggests the order in which you could tackle various types of models. It is best to proceed in easy stages to develop your skills of building and flying models.

1. Glider/rubber-powered plane made from sheet balsa.
2. Larger glider/rubber-powered model with tissue-covered framework construction.
3. Control-line trainer made of solid balsa or plastic.
4. Sheet balsa free-flight power model with small engine.
5. Framework power model, either control-line or free-flight.

It is a good idea to join your local aeromodelling club. The members will probably be happy to give you help and advice when you need it. It is also a good way of finding out about the more advanced types of models and of buying reliable second-hand equipment like engines. (Look on page 31 for more information about clubs.)

Control-line

A control-line model is always powered by a miniature engine. The model flies on two lines, in a circle round the pilot. The pilot can control its flight by pulling on the lines. One line makes the model climb, the other makes it dive.
(See pages 18-19 for more about control-lines.)

▲This is a trainer model, made from sheet balsa to withstand crashes. Trainers are the easiest models to pilot.

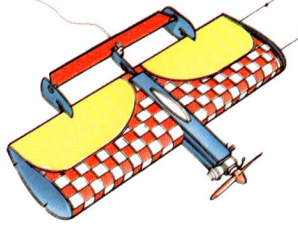

▲Two combat models are flown together. Each tows a streamer and the other plane tries to cut it down.

▲This is an aerobatic model which is designed to perform difficult manoeuvres in the air.

Radio-controlled

Radio-controlled models are the most sophisticated type. The pilot has a radio transmitter that sends command signals to a receiver inside the model. With this system you have complete control of your model's flight.
(See pages 22-23 for more about radio-control.)

▲A radio-controlled trainer is designed to be stable in flight so that it is simple for a learner to pilot.

▲Stunt planes are difficult to fly and can perform even more aerobatics than real, full-size aircraft.

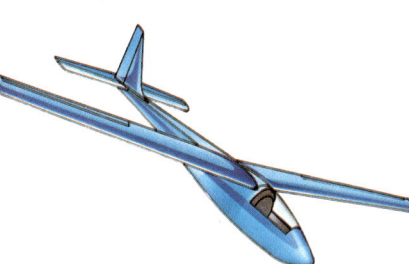

▲Radio-control gliders can be flown in distance, duration, or aerobatic competitions. They are often flown on hillsides.

Scale models

A scale model is a small replica of a real aircraft, made to look as much like the original as possible. Scale models are often quite heavy, because of the detail added to them. This means they fly best by radio-control or on control-lines.

▲This is a scale model. It resembles a real aircraft but cannot be an exact copy of the real thing.

▲Peanut scale models are very small rubber-powered planes. They must be light and are hard to make and fly.

▲Scale models are used in the aircraft industry to publicize airlines and air travel and to test new plane designs.

HOW PLANES FLY

Model aircraft fly in much the same way as full-size planes and are subject to the same laws of aerodynamics. These pages explain some of the principles of flight and show how models fly. The picture below shows a small powered sports model of the kind often used for free flight and radio-controlled flying. This type of design is very popular because it is stable in flight and quite simple to build.

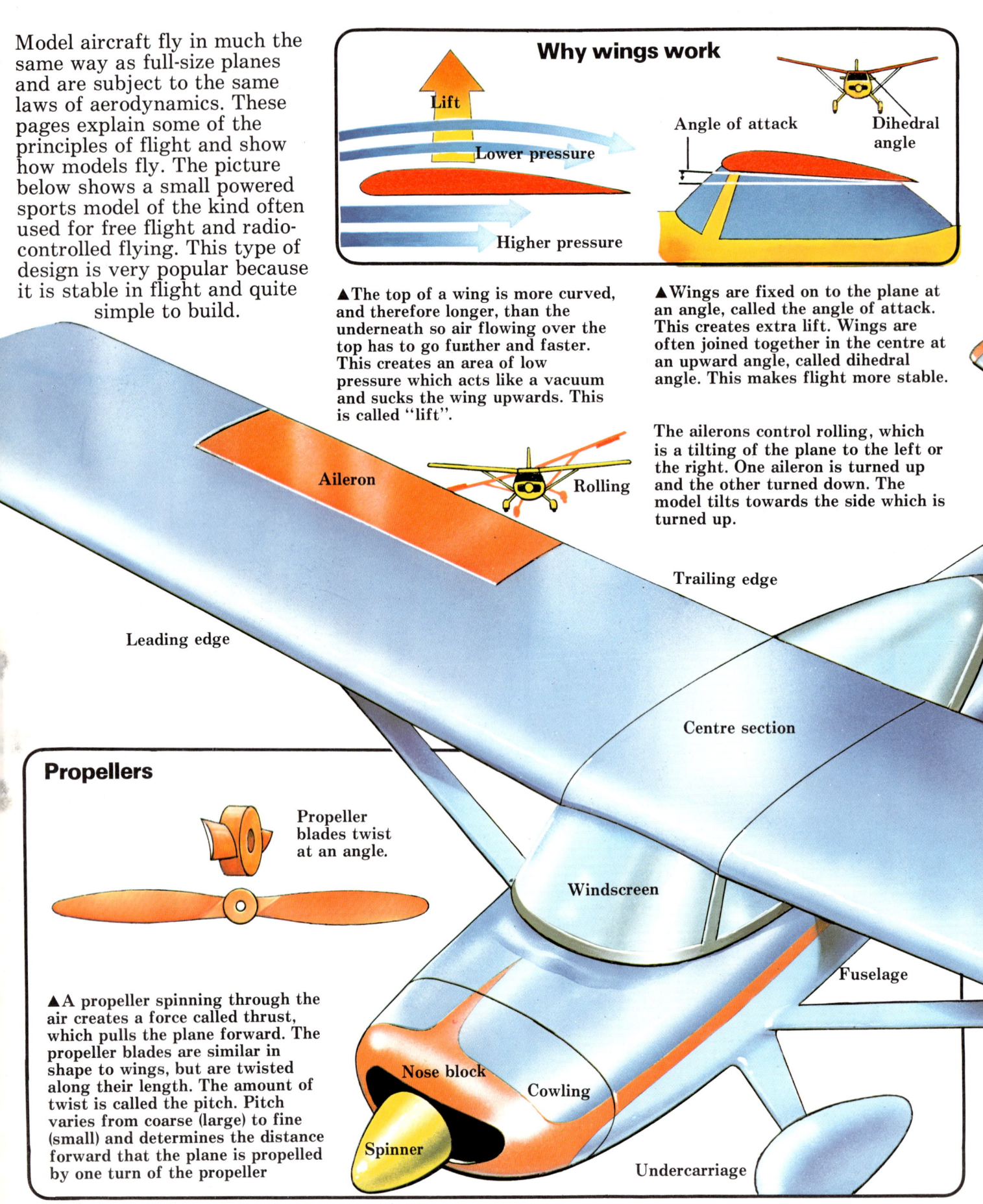

Why wings work

▲The top of a wing is more curved, and therefore longer, than the underneath so air flowing over the top has to go further and faster. This creates an area of low pressure which acts like a vacuum and sucks the wing upwards. This is called "lift".

▲Wings are fixed on to the plane at an angle, called the angle of attack. This creates extra lift. Wings are often joined together in the centre at an upward angle, called dihedral angle. This makes flight more stable.

The ailerons control rolling, which is a tilting of the plane to the left or the right. One aileron is turned up and the other turned down. The model tilts towards the side which is turned up.

Propellers

Propeller blades twist at an angle.

▲A propeller spinning through the air creates a force called thrust, which pulls the plane forward. The propeller blades are similar in shape to wings, but are twisted along their length. The amount of twist is called the pitch. Pitch varies from coarse (large) to fine (small) and determines the distance forward that the plane is propelled by one turn of the propeller

Yawing is the movement of the plane to left or right. It can be controlled by the rudder. To turn the plane to the right, set the rudder to the right. To turn it left, set the rudder to the left.

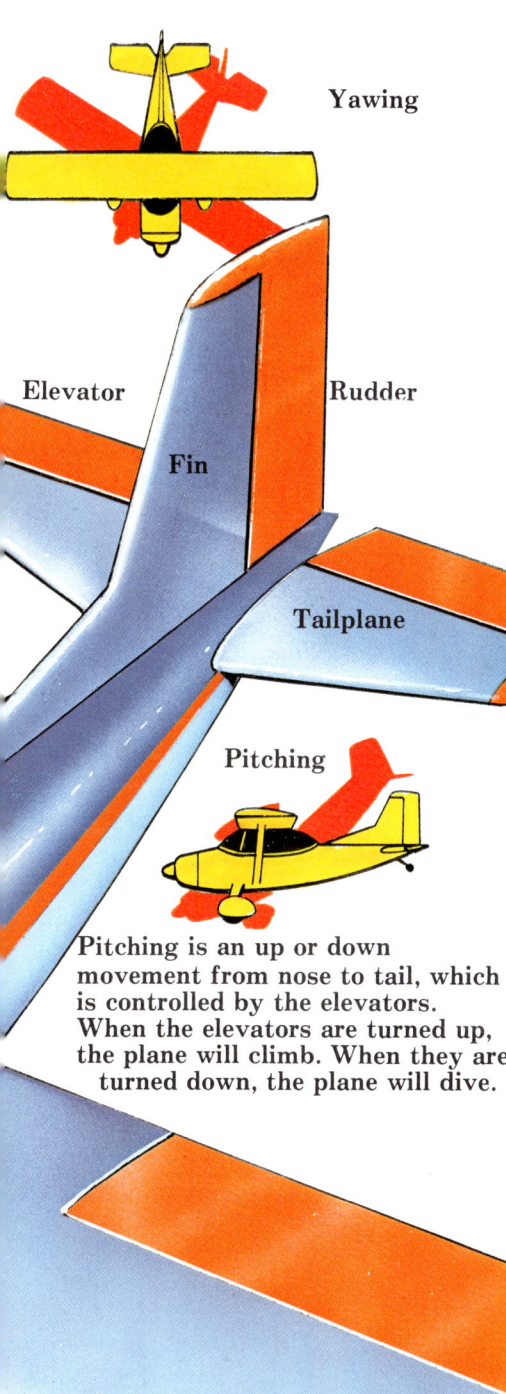

Pitching is an up or down movement from nose to tail, which is controlled by the elevators. When the elevators are turned up, the plane will climb. When they are turned down, the plane will dive.

The four forces of flight

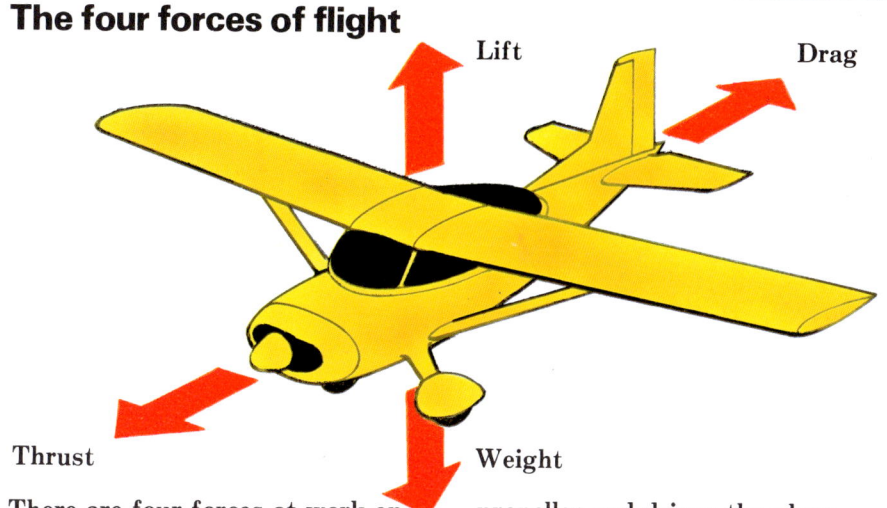

There are four forces at work on a plane in flight—weight, lift, thrust and drag. Weight is gravity pulling the plane down. This is counteracted by the lift produced when air flows over the wings. Thrust is provided by the spinning propeller and drives the plane forwards. The air resists this movement, and creates the force of drag. A plane can only fly level and steady when the weight equals lift and thrust equals drag.

The forces in action

▶When a model is taxiing, the weight is greater than lift so it remains on the ground. The model accelerates because the thrust is stronger than the drag. This makes air flow over the wings, which produces ever increasing lift.

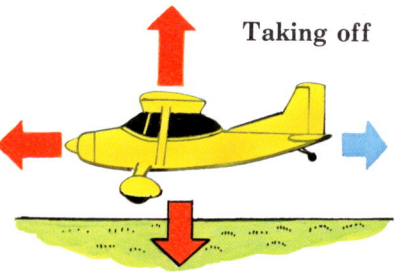

◀At a certain speed lift will equal weight. As soon as this speed is exceeded, lift becomes the stronger force. When this happens the model takes off from the ground and begins to climb.

▶A free-flight model will go on climbing until the engine stops. With radio-controlled or control-line planes you can balance the forces so that the model's flight will become level.

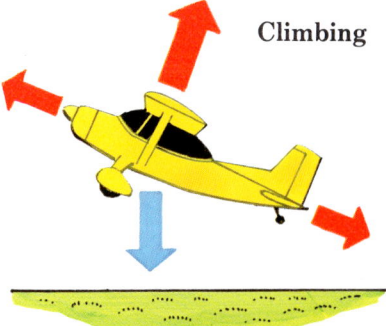

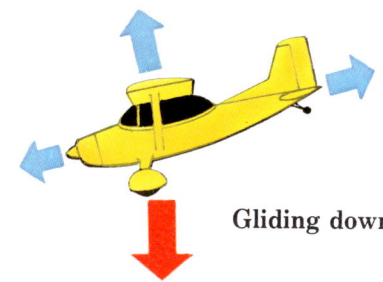

◀When the engine stops, the model glides. Although weight is the strongest force the model does not crash because the wings still produce lift. The increasing drag helps too as it limits the model's speed, making descent slower.

BUILDING WITH BALSA WOOD

These pages explain the stages that you will have to go through when you build a model aircraft. The pictures show a small rubber-powered plane being built from a kit, but the principles will be the same if you are making a glider or any sort of framework model. A kit will contain all the materials you need but not the tools, which you can buy separately from a model shop. The picture and lists on the right show the materials and tools you will need.

Materials.
1. Sheet balsa wood
2. Strip balsa wood
3. Balsa glue
4. Tissue paper
5. Tissue paste
6. Dope
7. Dope thinners

Tools.
8. Craft knife
9. Long pins
10. Drawing pins
11. Soft brushes
12. Sand paper (wrapped round block of wood)
13. Elastic bands

1

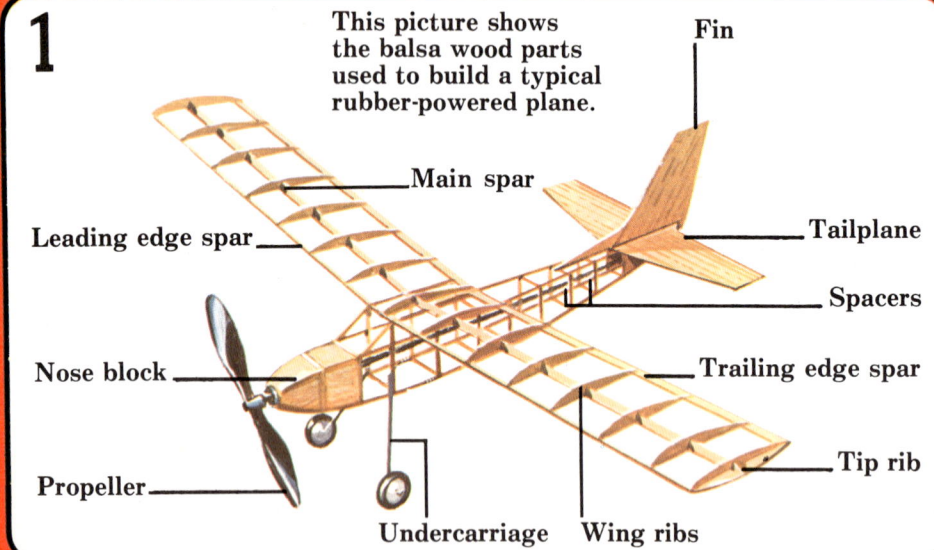

This picture shows the balsa wood parts used to build a typical rubber-powered plane.

Labels: Fin, Main spar, Tailplane, Leading edge spar, Spacers, Nose block, Trailing edge spar, Propeller, Tip rib, Undercarriage, Wing ribs

2

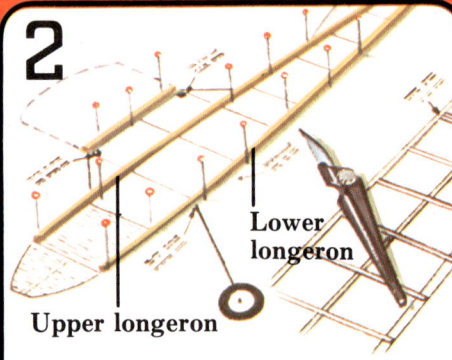

Labels: Upper longeron, Lower longeron

▲Read the instructions and plan carefully. Pin the plan down to keep it steady and cover with some clear polythene to protect it from glue. Pin the longerons in place on the plan, as shown in this picture above.

3

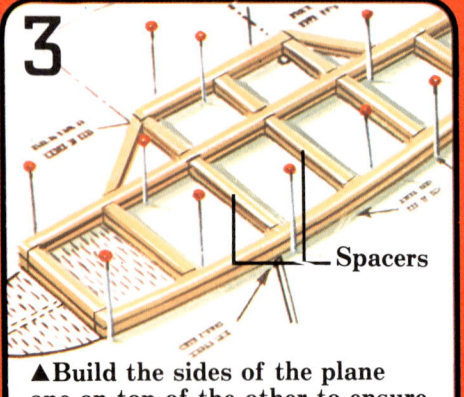

Spacers

▲Build the sides of the plane one on top of the other to ensure that they are the same size. Cut the spacers in pairs, so they are exactly the same length for each side and then glue them into place between the longerons.

4

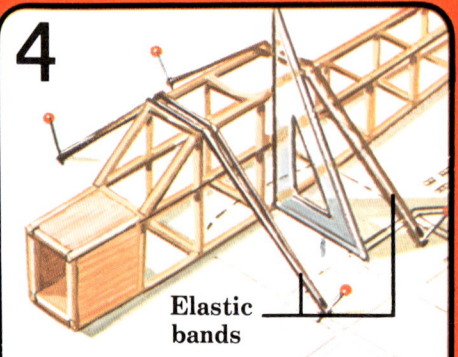

Elastic bands

▲Ease the sides apart when dry and stand them upright on the plan. Glue the upper and lower spacers into position. Leave the fuselage to dry, held straight and upright by pins and elastic bands.

5

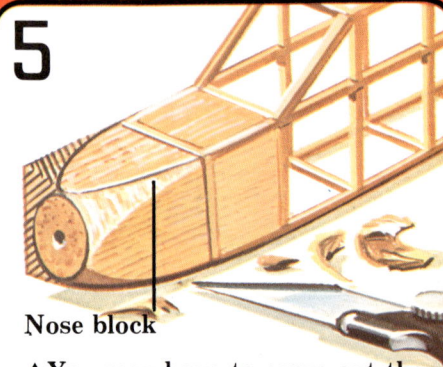

Nose block

▲You may have to carve out the nose block yourself. Draw the shape shown on the plan onto a block of balsa wood. Carve it out with a sharp craft knife and use sandpaper to get a smooth finish and shape.

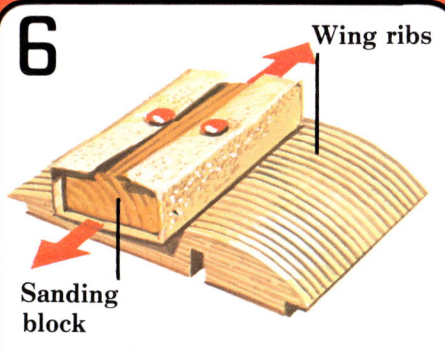

6 Wing ribs / Sanding block

▲If the wing ribs are all the same size, cut and sand them together in a block as shown here. If the ribs are all different sizes you will have to cut them out and sand them to shape separately.

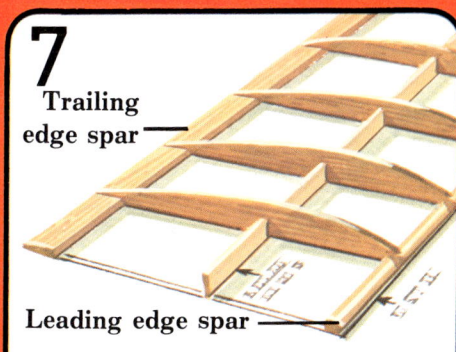

7 Trailing edge spar / Leading edge spar

▲The wings are constructed in a similar way to the fuselage. First pin the spars into place on the plan. Position the trailing edge and then stick on the ribs, making sure they are positioned at right angles.

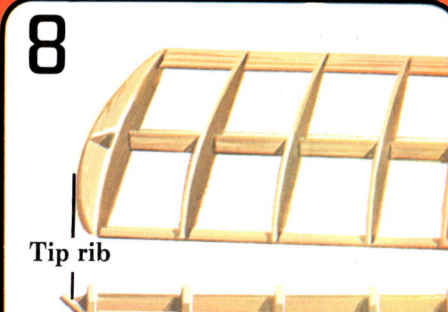

8 Tip rib

▲The leading-edge spar and wing-tip rib are glued into place last. The tip rib is usually positioned at a special angle, indicated on the plan. Now sand all the balsa to a smooth finish with the sanding block.

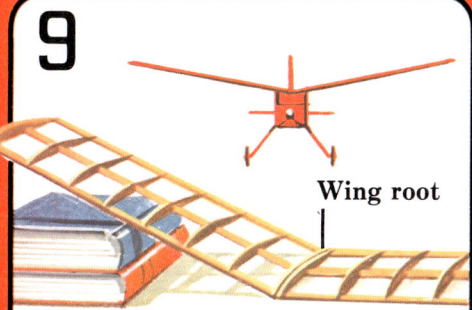

9 Wing root

▲Most wings are built in two sections which are glued together in a "V" shape to form a dihedral angle. The root ribs must be placed at the angle shown on the plan. Support the wing when drying.

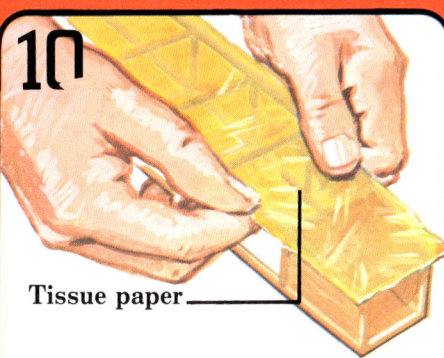

10 Tissue paper

▲Cut the tissue slightly too big. Apply tissue paste to the frame and lay the tissue over it. Stick down the short edges first. Gently smooth out any wrinkles from side to side. Trim the tissue to size when it is dry.

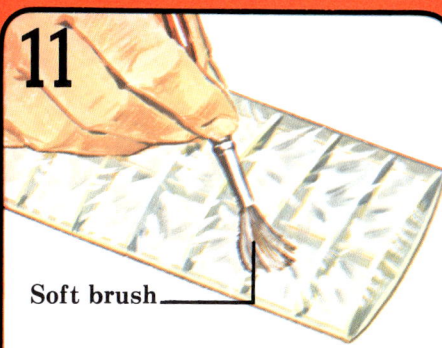

11 Soft brush

▲The tissue has to be shrunk onto the frame to give a tight strong finish. Lightly brush or spray water over the tissue surface. When this is dry apply several coats of dope thinned with dope thinners.

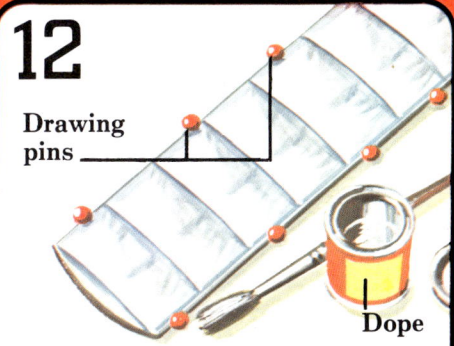

12 Drawing pins / Dope

▲When you shrink and dope the wings, tailplane or any part that could warp, leave it to dry pinned down flat with drawing pins. Treat warps by re-doping and pinning down the affected part to dry again.

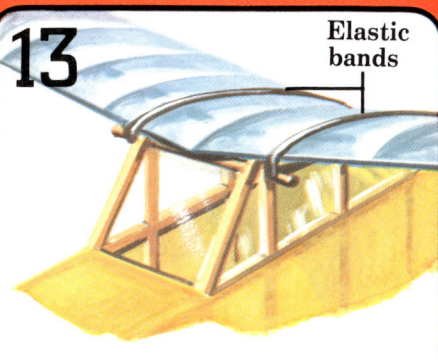

13 Elastic bands

▲When it has dried, the model can be assembled. The wings are often fixed to the fuselage with elastic bands, as this makes them less likely to be damaged in a crash and much easier to adjust for trimming.

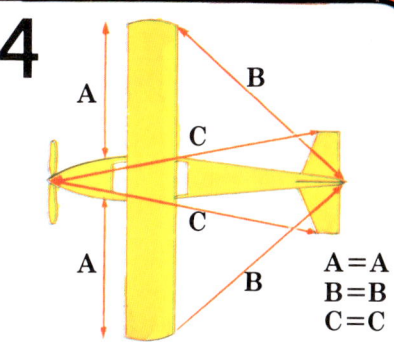

14 A=A, B=B, C=C

▲A model will only fly well if it is carefully made. Check that the dimensions shown above are equal by measuring them with some thread. Look at your model from all angles to check that there are no warps.

FIRST FLIGHTS

Every free-flight model has to go through a very important process, known as trimming, before it will fly really well. This involves testing the model's flight and making small adjustments to it so that it will fly better.

These pages explain how to test and trim free-flight models to prevent problems such as stalling and diving during flight.

If you have built a rubber- or engine-powered model you must first test-fly it without any power. Only after it can glide properly should you test and trim its flight under power.

Test flight

▲All free-flight models should be test glided to see how they fly—even powered models. This picture shows a test launch and the three possible flight paths that a model could take.

Launch the model into the wind from a kneeling position. Throw it

Balance

▼Every model has a balance point called the centre of gravity, or C of G for short. If suspended from this point a model should hang level without tilting up or down.

Most kits and plans indicate where the centre of gravity should be on a finished model and the first thing to test on a new model is that it hangs level. The two pictures below show how to carry out this balance test on a free-flight model. You need some string and two pins.

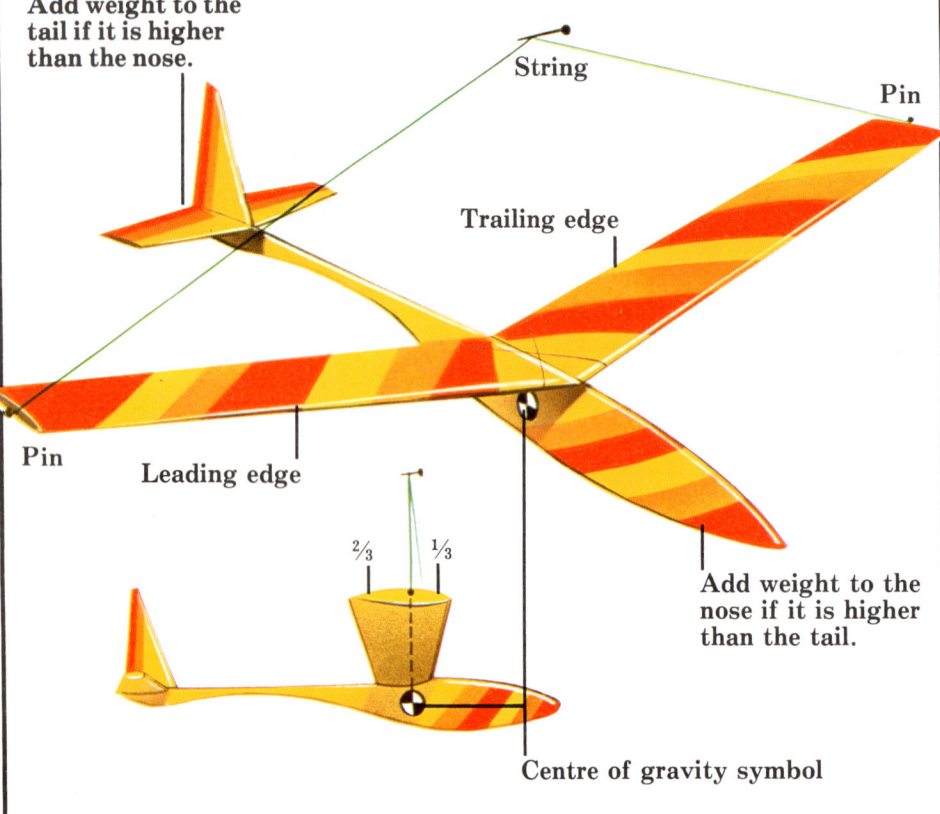

▲On most free-flight models the centre of gravity is at a point in the middle of the fuselage, about one third of the way back from the leading edge of the wing. The easiest way to balance the plane is to hang it on a length of string, pinned to the wing tips at the same distance back from the leading edge as the centre of gravity (see small picture).

If the model does not hang level, add some weight to the high end. Try using rolled up empty glue tubes or plasticine for extra weight.

Trimming gliding flight

If your model dives on a test glide you may have launched it too gently and slowly. Test it again. If it still dives try *one* of the following adjustments and then re-test its flight.

1 Increase weight at the tail end, the model could be a little nose heavy.

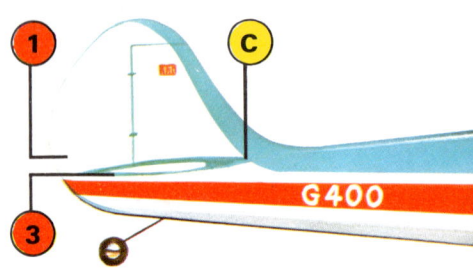

2 Create extra lift by increasing the angle of attack of the wings. To do this insert a small amount of scrap balsa between the fuselage and the leading edge of the wing.

3 Insert some balsa under the trailing edge of the tailplane.

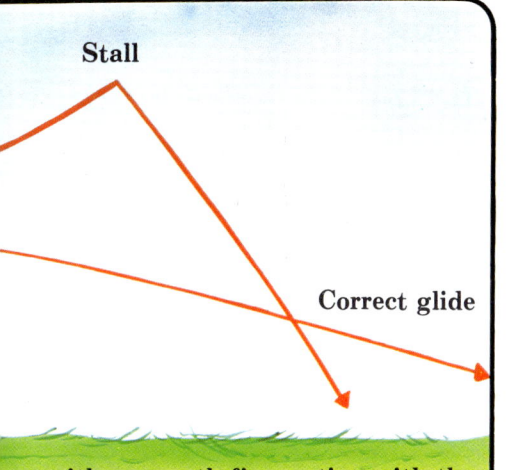

Stall

Correct glide

with a smooth firm action with the nose pointing slightly down and the wings level. When the model is correctly trimmed it will fly in a gentle flat glide. The following sections show you how to correct stalling and diving on gliding and powered flight.

If your model stalls on a test glide you may have launched it too hard and too quickly. Test it again. If it still stalls try *one* of the following adjustments and re-test the model's flight.

A Increase weight at the nose end, the model could be a little tail heavy.

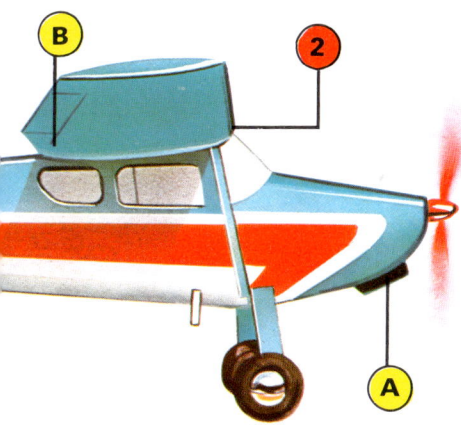

B Decrease lift by changing the angle of attack. To do this insert a small amount of scrap balsa between the fuselage and the trailing edge of the wing.

C Insert some balsa under the leading edge of the tailplane.

Trimming powered flight

Once a powered model is gliding properly, start the engine following the instructions supplied and then test the model's flight under power. Keep the test flights short and if possible make the engine run slowly. If the engine speed is not adjustable, put the propeller on back to front as this will reduce the power.

The propeller creates thrust when it spins and it is the angle of thrust which may cause the plane to dive or stall when it is flying under power. The next section shows how to change the angle.

Down-thrust

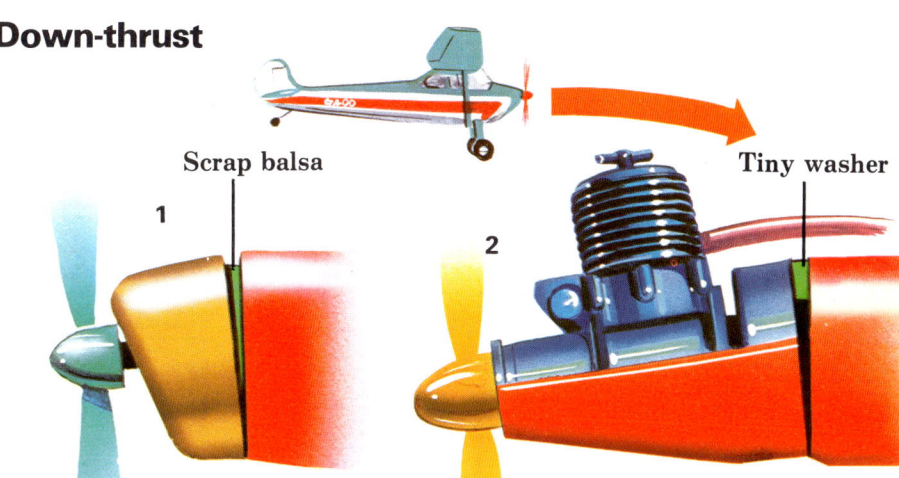

Scrap balsa Tiny washer

▲If a powered model dives the propeller is probably creating too much down-thrust. If it stalls there is probably not enough down-thrust. The degree of down-thrust can be changed by altering the angle at which the propeller is fixed to the fuselage.

Picture number one above shows how to increase down-thrust on a rubber-powered plane by sticking some scrap balsa behind the nose block.

Picture number two shows how to increase down-thrust on a powered model by putting tiny washers under the appropriate pair of mounting screws on the engine.

Right-thrust

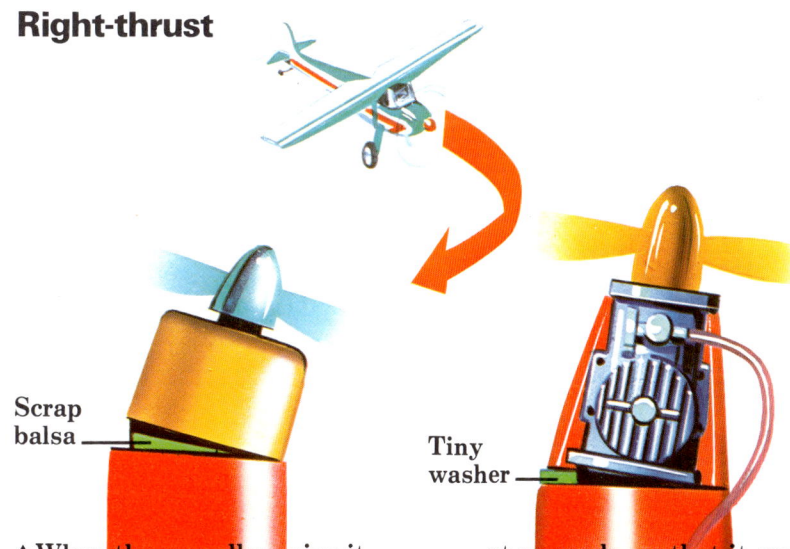

Scrap balsa Tiny washer

▲When the propeller spins it makes the body of the plane try to turn round in the opposite direction. This is called "torque". If your model tips over onto one side when it is flying under power, it might be because of the torque.

This problem can be corrected by fixing the propeller to the fuselage at an angle, so that it creates thrust to the right.

Most models are designed with built-in side-thrust but you may have to alter it. The two pictures above show how to do this on a rubber-powered and an engine powered plane.

MODEL GLIDERS

Gliders, which are also known as sailplanes or soarers, are motorless aircraft designed to float through the air, carried by breezes and thermals. A thermal is a rising current of warm air, caused by heat reflected from the ground. Thermals often occur over tarmac, concrete or sandy surfaces.

Model gliders are usually built to fly well rather than look realistic. They vary in design from the most simple hand-launched gliders which make excellent first projects, to the very sophisticated designs which are flown in international competitions. (See page 23 for radio-controlled gliders.)

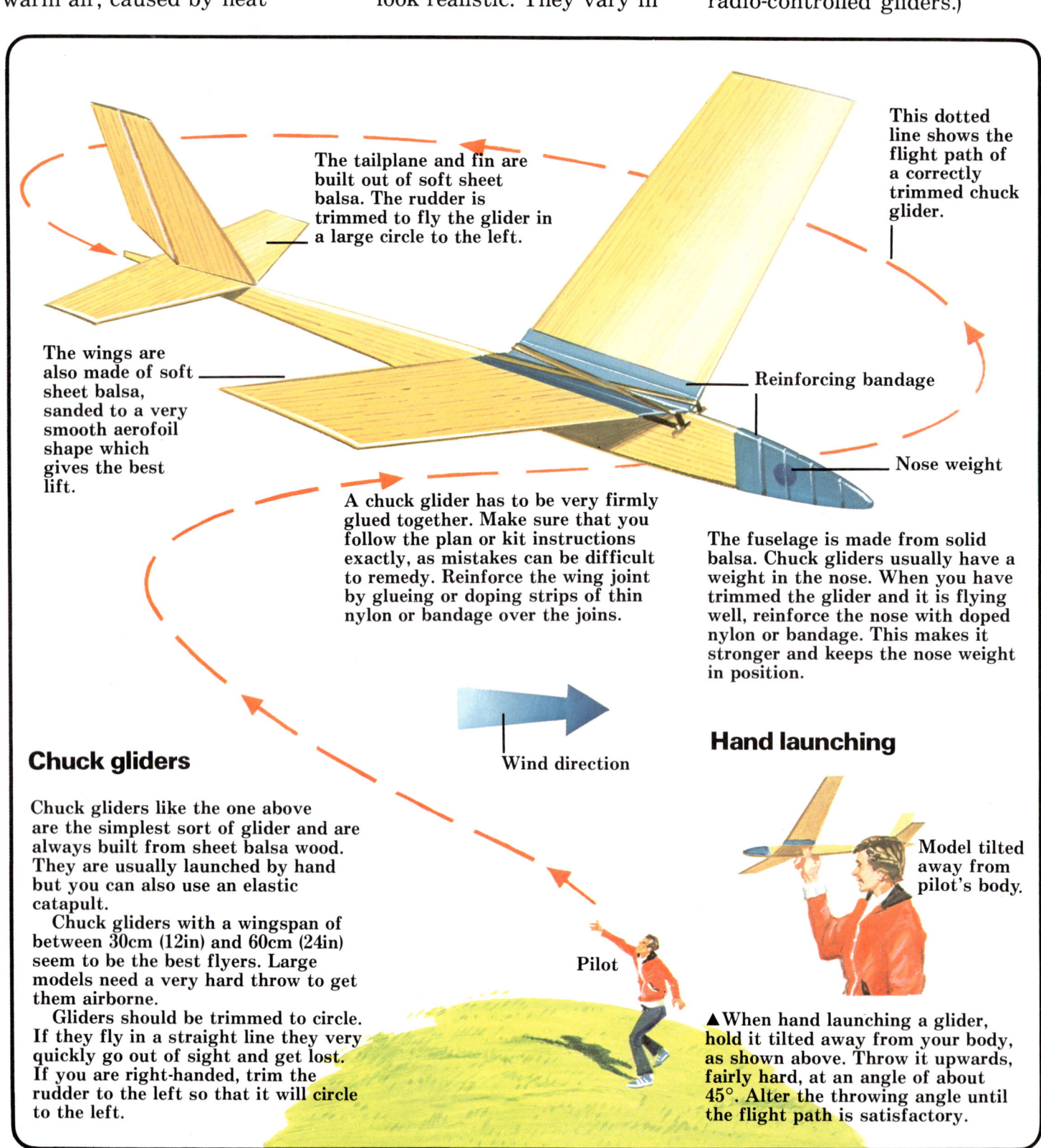

The tailplane and fin are built out of soft sheet balsa. The rudder is trimmed to fly the glider in a large circle to the left.

This dotted line shows the flight path of a correctly trimmed chuck glider.

The wings are also made of soft sheet balsa, sanded to a very smooth aerofoil shape which gives the best lift.

Reinforcing bandage

Nose weight

A chuck glider has to be very firmly glued together. Make sure that you follow the plan or kit instructions exactly, as mistakes can be difficult to remedy. Reinforce the wing joint by glueing or doping strips of thin nylon or bandage over the joins.

The fuselage is made from solid balsa. Chuck gliders usually have a weight in the nose. When you have trimmed the glider and it is flying well, reinforce the nose with doped nylon or bandage. This makes it stronger and keeps the nose weight in position.

Wind direction

Chuck gliders

Chuck gliders like the one above are the simplest sort of glider and are always built from sheet balsa wood. They are usually launched by hand but you can also use an elastic catapult.

Chuck gliders with a wingspan of between 30cm (12in) and 60cm (24in) seem to be the best flyers. Large models need a very hard throw to get them airborne.

Gliders should be trimmed to circle. If they fly in a straight line they very quickly go out of sight and get lost. If you are right-handed, trim the rudder to the left so that it will **circle** to the left.

Pilot

Hand launching

Model tilted away from pilot's body.

▲When hand launching a glider, **hold it tilted away from your body, as shown above.** Throw it upwards, **fairly hard, at an angle of about 45°.** Alter the throwing angle until the flight path is satisfactory.

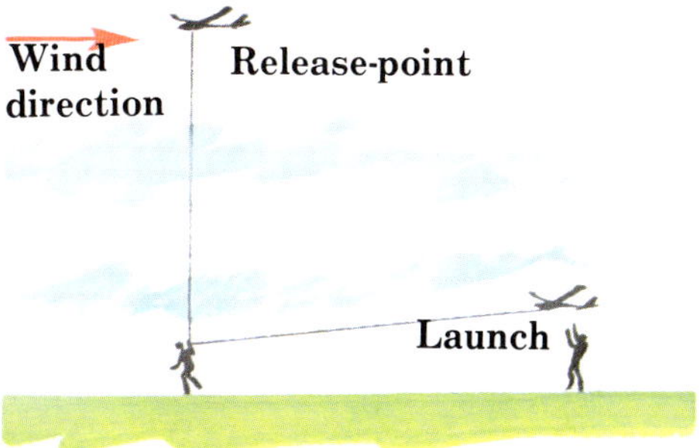

Tow-line gliders

▲ As the name suggests, tow-line gliders are launched by being towed up into the air on a line. It takes two people to launch this kind of glider. One holds the model while the other runs with the line, towing the plane into the air like a kite. The tow-line is released once the glider is flying well. The picture above shows a typical launch.

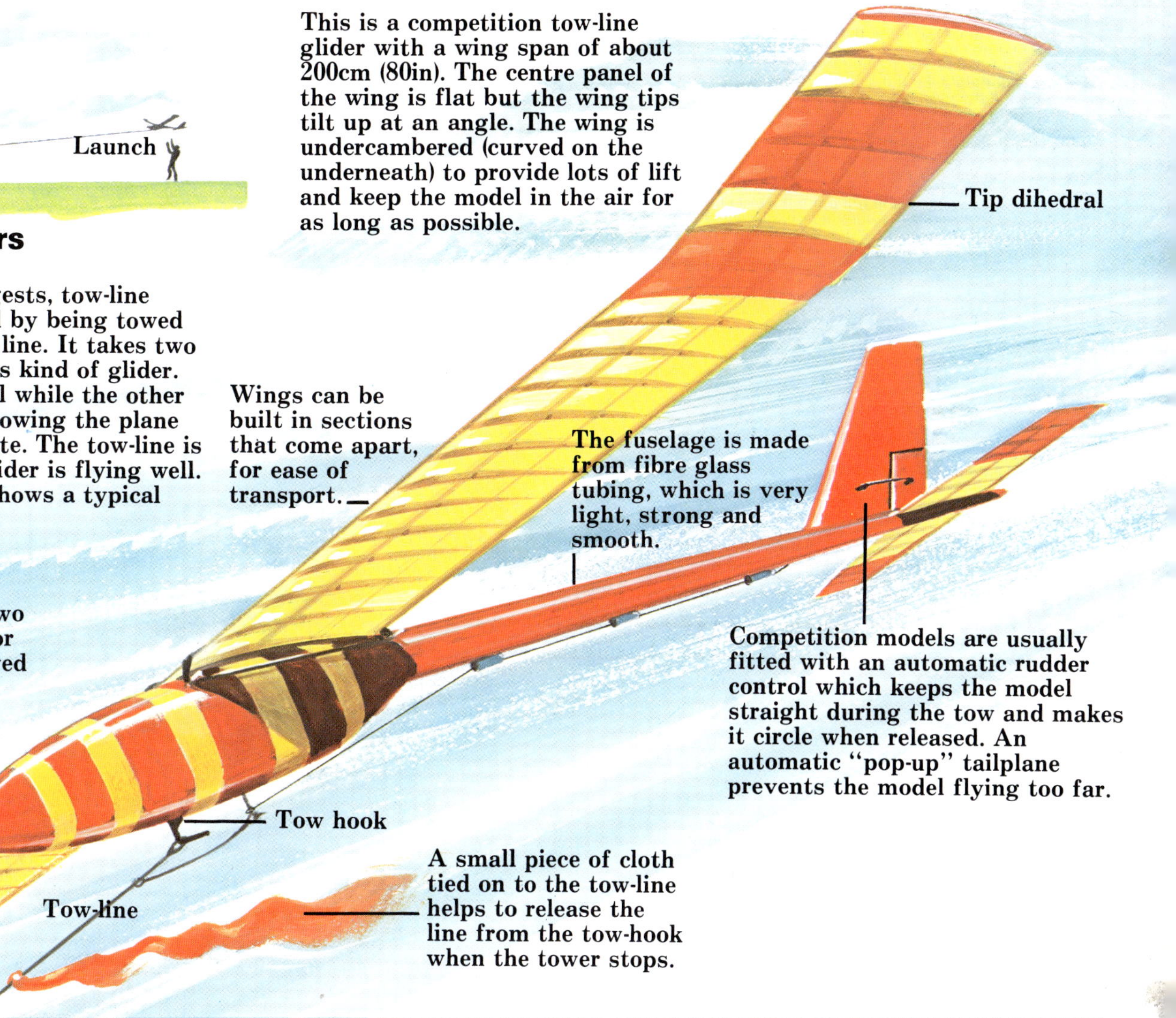

Most gliders have two or three tow hooks or one that can be moved to suit weather and flying conditions.

Wings can be built in sections that come apart, for ease of transport.

This is a competition tow-line glider with a wing span of about 200cm (80in). The centre panel of the wing is flat but the wing tips tilt up at an angle. The wing is undercambered (curved on the underneath) to provide lots of lift and keep the model in the air for as long as possible.

Tip dihedral

The fuselage is made from fibre glass tubing, which is very light, strong and smooth.

Competition models are usually fitted with an automatic rudder control which keeps the model straight during the tow and makes it circle when released. An automatic "pop-up" tailplane prevents the model flying too far.

Tow hook

A small piece of cloth tied on to the tow-line helps to release the line from the tow-hook when the tower stops.

Tow-line

Automatic controls

If they are not controlled, gliders may travel a great distance and remain in the air for a long time. This is not very convenient, so pre-set automatic controls can be fitted to regulate the model's flight.

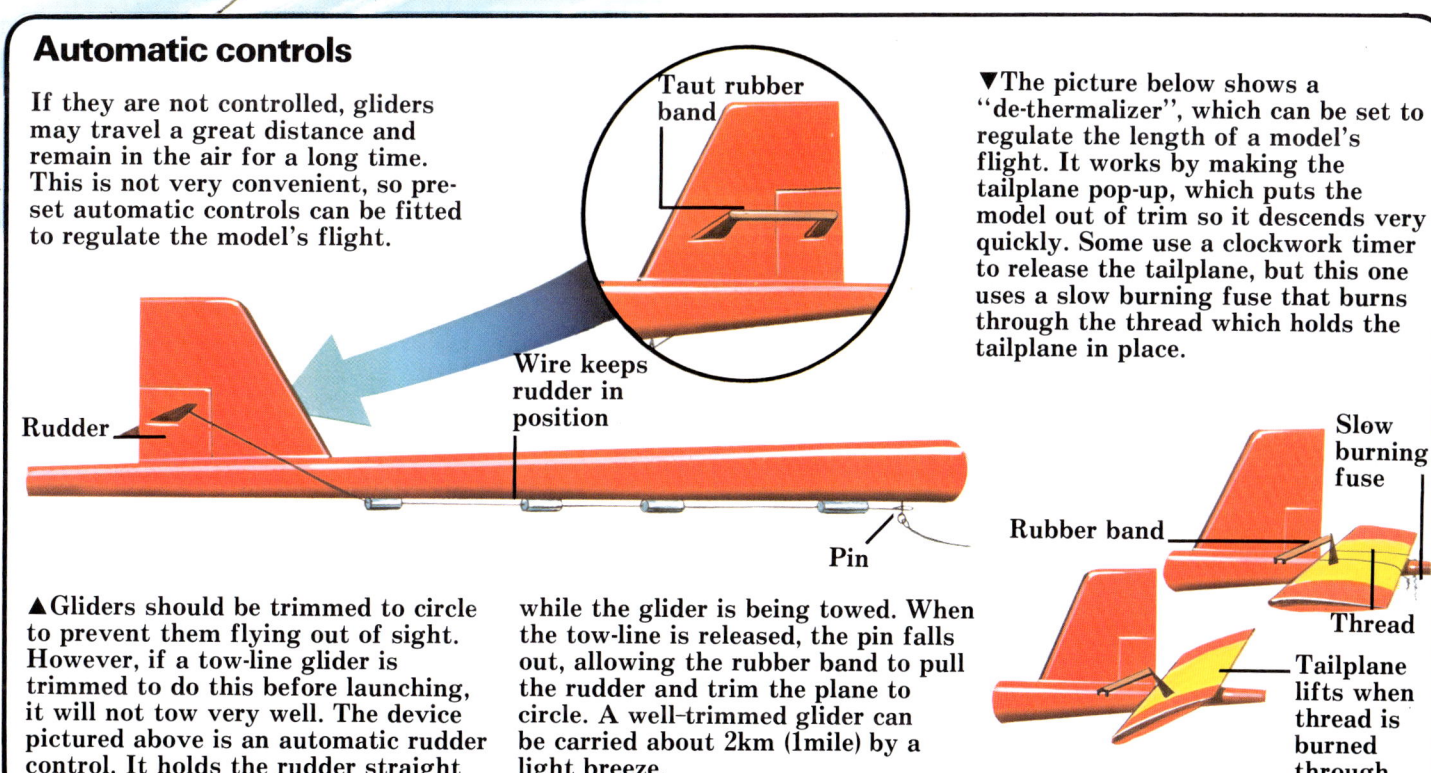

▼ The picture below shows a "de-thermalizer", which can be set to regulate the length of a model's flight. It works by making the tailplane pop-up, which puts the model out of trim so it descends very quickly. Some use a clockwork timer to release the tailplane, but this one uses a slow burning fuse that burns through the thread which holds the tailplane in place.

▲ Gliders should be trimmed to circle to prevent them flying out of sight. However, if a tow-line glider is trimmed to do this before launching, it will not tow very well. The device pictured above is an automatic rudder control. It holds the rudder straight while the glider is being towed. When the tow-line is released, the pin falls out, allowing the rubber band to pull the rudder and trim the plane to circle. A well-trimmed glider can be carried about 2km (1mile) by a light breeze.

RUBBER-POWERED PLANES

Rubber-driven planes can be the simplest kind of powered model to build and to fly. They are often similar in construction to gliders. Some are fitted with wheels and can take off from the ground, as long as it is firm and flat.

Although the motors are made out of rubber strip, they need almost as much care and attention as a miniature engine. Always treat the rubber carefully and throw it away when it shows any signs of wear or damage. If a wound-up motor breaks or comes untied it can easily wreck a model so make your motors carefully.

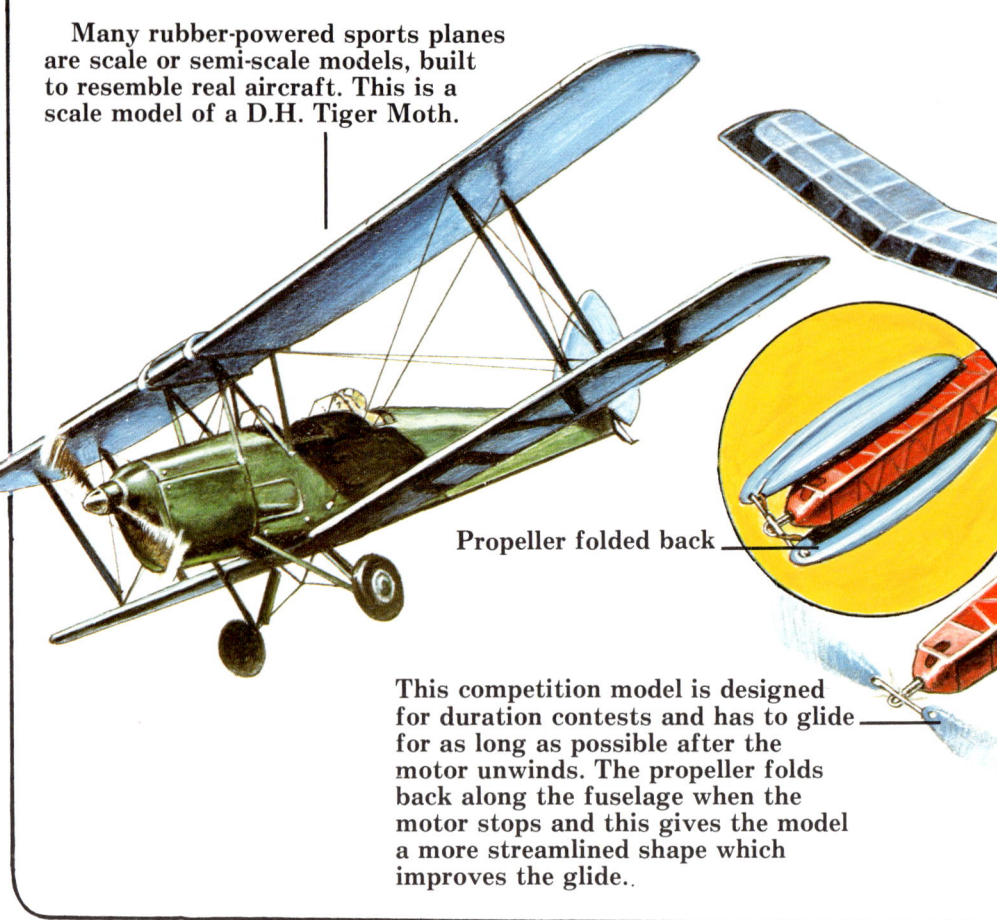

Many rubber-powered sports planes are scale or semi-scale models, built to resemble real aircraft. This is a scale model of a D.H. Tiger Moth.

Propeller folded back

This competition model is designed for duration contests and has to glide for as long as possible after the motor unwinds. The propeller folds back along the fuselage when the motor stops and this gives the model a more streamlined shape which improves the glide.

Making a motor

You need a surprisingly long rubber motor to make your model fly for more than a very short time. The pictures below show how to make an efficient rubber motor. Your kit or plan will recommend what size and length of rubber strip to use.

Drill chuck

▲Winding a rubber motor by hand is very slow and tiring. Make a motor winder by fitting a hook into the chuck of a small hand drill. You can make a hook from wire or buy a hook like a cup-hook. You need to be able to count the number of times you wind the motor. To do this easily, put a mark on the chuck and see how many times it goes round in one turn of the drill handle. Now work out how many turns of the handle will wind the rubber 50 and 100 times. Your kit will tell you how many times to wind the motor.

▲Cut your strip of rubber about four times as long as the plane's fuselage.

Bind with cotton thread

▲Tie the rubber strip into a single loop, making the join with a reef knot and tying down the ends as shown above.

Rub the motor with some rubber lubricant as this helps to preserve the rubber. The motor now has to be "pre-tensioned" so that it is tight enough to hold in the nose block.

▲If a motor is not pre-tensioned the nose will fall out as the motor unwinds.

It takes two people to pre-tension a rubber motor, so find someone to help you.

▲First take the loop and wind it anti-clockwise a few times. Your helper holds one end while you wind at the other end, using the drill as a motor winder.

Now fold the wound-up loop in two. The two halves will twirl-up together. The rubber motor will now be about the same length as the plane.

Elastic bands

▲The last step is to wind-up the rubber again, until it is just shorter than the fuselage. Bind the two ends with elastic bands so that it will not come undone.

The motor is now ready to be fitted inside the model.

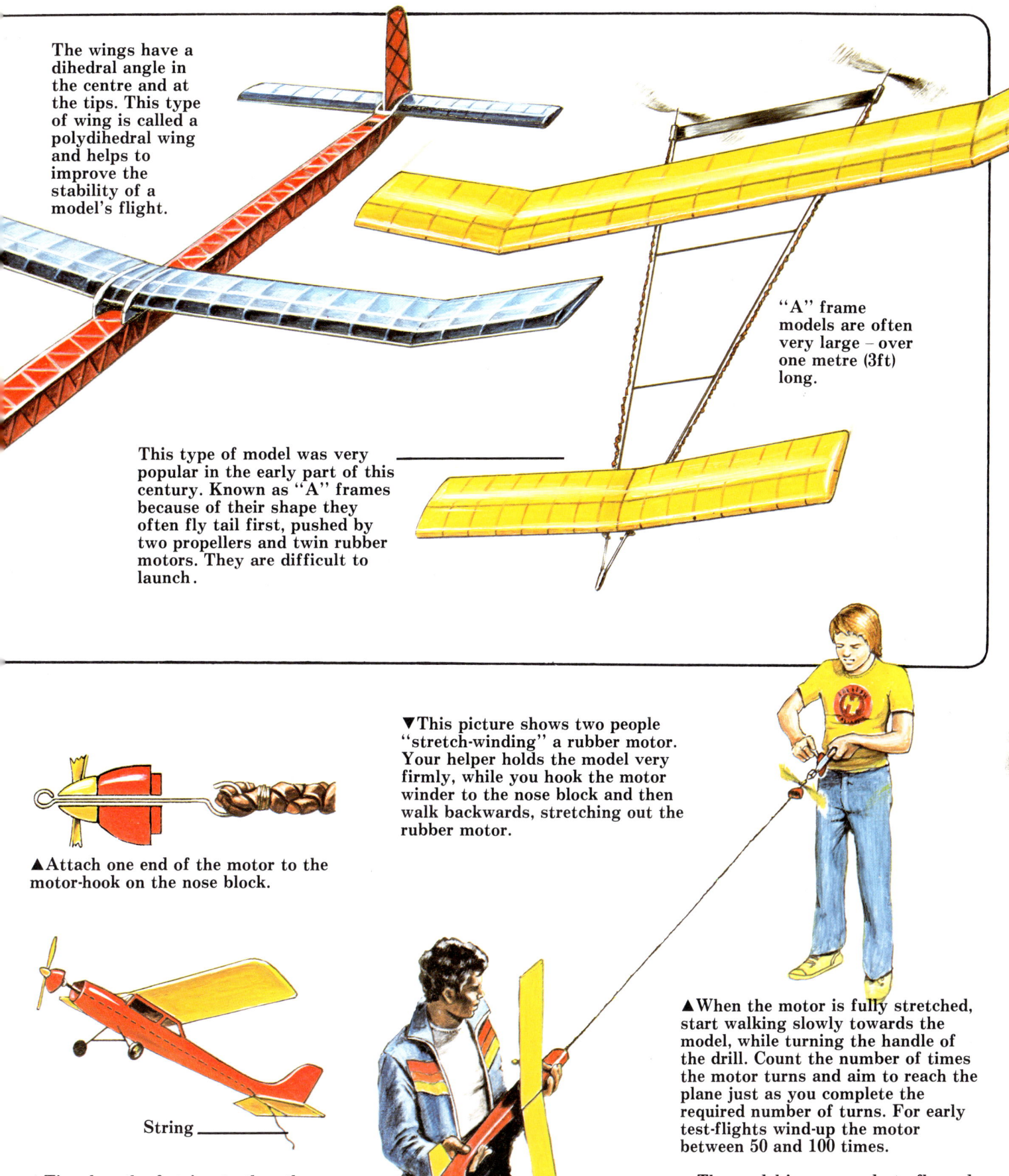

The wings have a dihedral angle in the centre and at the tips. This type of wing is called a polydihedral wing and helps to improve the stability of a model's flight.

This type of model was very popular in the early part of this century. Known as "A" frames because of their shape they often fly tail first, pushed by two propellers and twin rubber motors. They are difficult to launch.

"A" frame models are often very large – over one metre (3ft) long.

▲Attach one end of the motor to the motor-hook on the nose block.

▼This picture shows two people "stretch-winding" a rubber motor. Your helper holds the model very firmly, while you hook the motor winder to the nose block and then walk backwards, stretching out the rubber motor.

▲Tie a length of string to the other end of the motor. This will help you to pull it through the plane. Secure the motor in place with the motor peg at the tail end and the model is ready to be wound-up and launched.

▲When the motor is fully stretched, start walking slowly towards the model, while turning the handle of the drill. Count the number of times the motor turns and aim to reach the plane just as you complete the required number of turns. For early test-flights wind-up the motor between 50 and 100 times.

The model is now ready to fly and can be hand-launched or allowed to rise from the ground if it has wheels and the surface is suitable. Remember to trim the rudder so that the model will fly in circles.

MODEL ENGINES

Model aircraft engines are used to turn the plane's propeller. The three most common kinds of engine are the diesel, glowplug and CO_2 (carbon dioxide) engines. All three work on similar mechanical principles, but use different fuels in different ways.

Diesel and glowplug motors are both internal combustion engines, so called because they burn (combust) a mixture of fuel and air inside a cylinder. CO_2 engines are powered by pressurized carbon dioxide gas which does not burn.

4 The piston is joined to the crankshaft by the connecting rod. This converts the up and down motion of the piston to a circular movement that spins the propeller.

Diesel engine

1 The compression screw controls the pressure of the gas inside the cylinder. Set the screw as directed by the instructions with your engine.

The needle valve controls the amount of fuel in the fuel/air mixture.

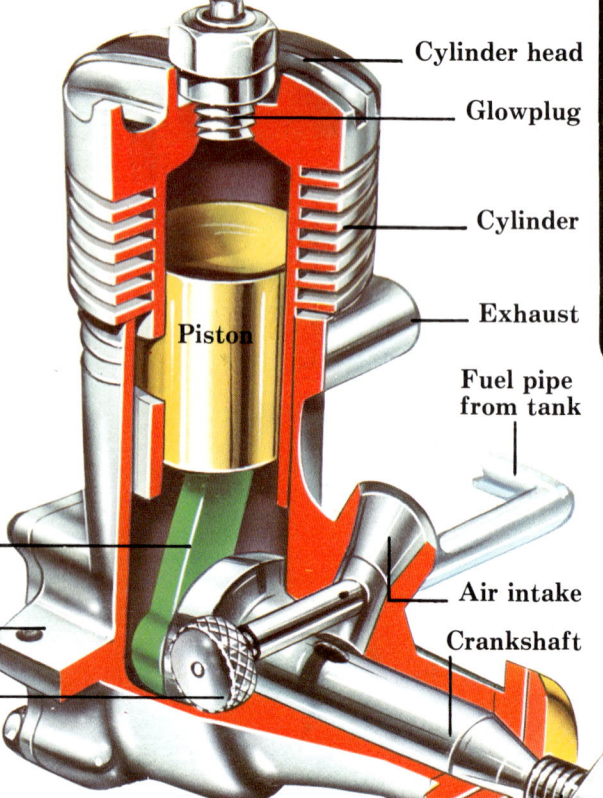

2 Air from the air intake and fuel from the fuel pipe, mix together. This forms the gassy mixture that is ignited to power the engine.

3 When the piston moves up it pushes the fuel/air mixture to the top of the cylinder. When the gas is very compressed it becomes hot enough to ignite and make the engine start.

The main difference between diesel and glowplug engines is in the way they ignite the fuel/air mixture inside the cylinder.

Diesel engines ignite the gassy mixture by squeezing it between the piston and the contra-piston. The mixture becomes very compressed and gets hot enough to burn.

Glowplug engines have a small coil of platinum wire inside the cylinder head, which gets hot when connected to a battery. This ignites the fuel/air mixture when it is compressed by the piston.

In both cases the burning mixture expands and pushes the piston down and this turns the propeller.

Glowplug engine

1 Glowplug engines have a tiny coil of platinum wire inside the cylinder head. This is called the glowplug or glowhead. When it is connected to the battery it gets hot and starts to glow, rather like an electric fire.

2 The glowing coil ignites the compressed fuel/air mixture inside the cylinder. The gas burns and expands, pushing the piston down.

3 Once the engine is running, the battery can be disconnected. The plug will continue to glow and ignite the gas.

4 Turning the needle valve changes the amount of fuel in the fuel/air mixture. Set the valve according to instructions with the engine. A mixture with a lot of fuel in it is called "rich", with a little fuel, it is called "lean".

5 As in the diesel engine, the piston is joined to the crankshaft by the connecting rod. This converts the up and down motion of the piston to a circular movement that spins the propeller.

FLYING ON CONTROL-LINES

If you want to learn to fly on control-lines it is a good idea to start with a trainer model. Trainers are easier to pilot than ordinary models as they are less responsive to control. They are made from solid balsa or plastic to be extra strong as all learners have a few crashes. When you can keep a model on a level flight path try some more advanced piloting such as speed flying, combat, racing or aerobatics. (Look on page 24 for some control-line stunts.)

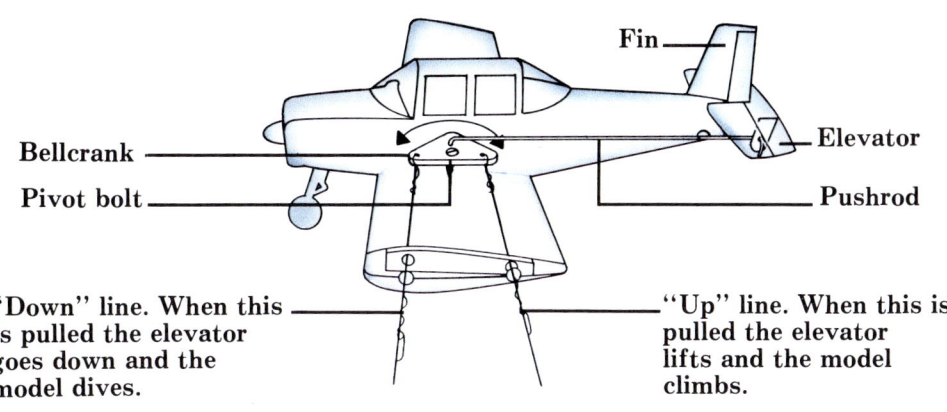

"Down" line. When this is pulled the elevator goes down and the model dives.

"Up" line. When this is pulled the elevator lifts and the model climbs.

▲This picture shows how the control-line system works. The flying lines are fixed to a bellcrank inside the plane. When either up or down line is pulled, the bellcrank swings on the pivot bolt. A length of wire, called the pushrod, joins the bellcrank to the elevator. So, when the bellcrank swings it moves the pushrod and the elevator, making the plane climb or dive.

Control-line scale model

This control-line plane is a scale model of an American low wing mono-plane, the Shinn 2150. Control-lines are particularly good for scale models as the planes can be heavier than a similar size free-flight model. This means that the model can be more detailed and realistic.

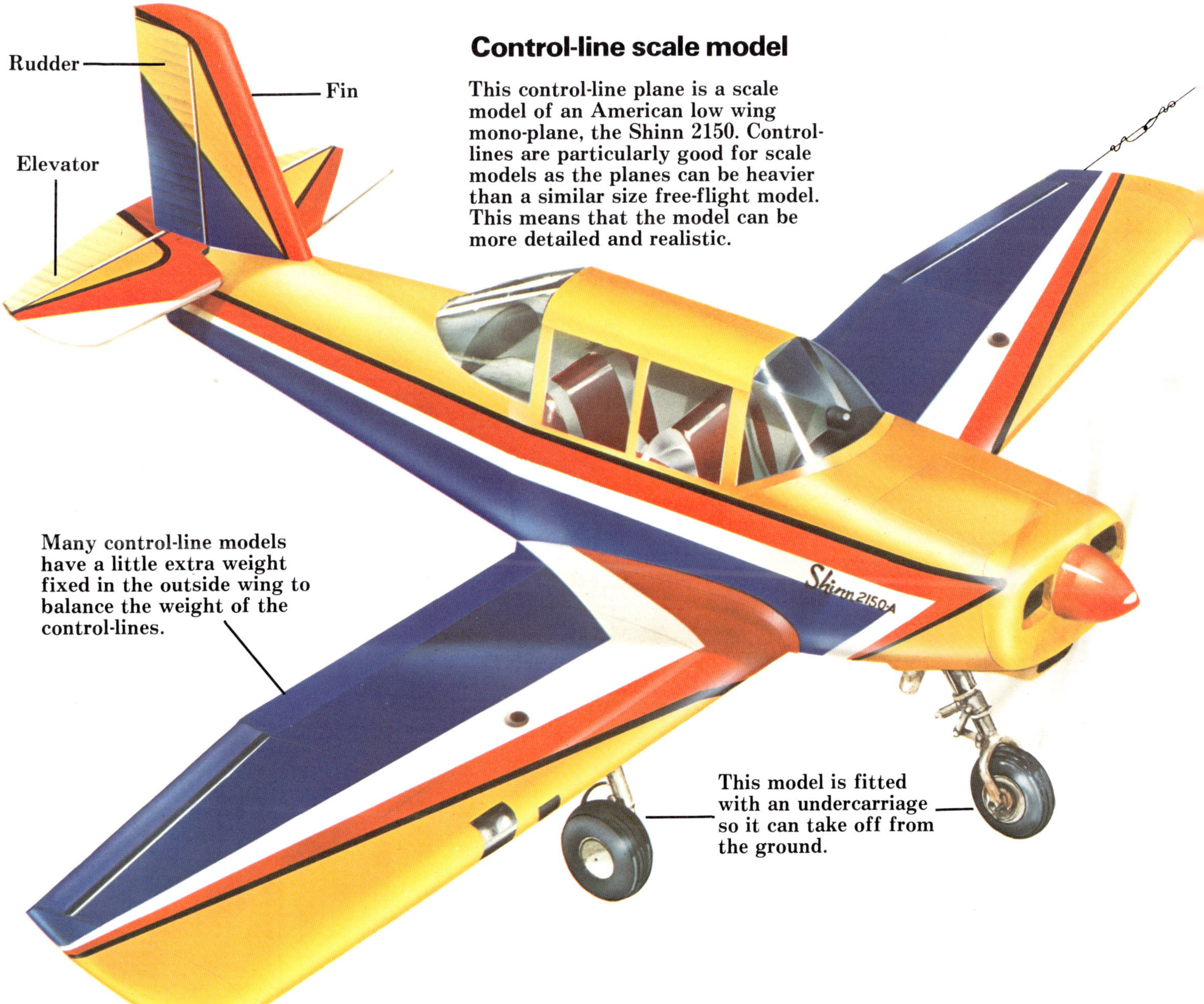

Many control-line models have a little extra weight fixed in the outside wing to balance the weight of the control-lines.

This model is fitted with an undercarriage so it can take off from the ground.

Competition flyers

The wings are mounted on a pylon to lift them higher. This kind of wing gives the model extra stability.

The wings are tilted upwards in the centre and at the tips. This is called a polydihedral wing.

Free-flight competition models are very sophisticated and specialized flying machines. They are designed to remain airborne for as long as possible after a very short engine run of ten seconds or less. The engine is stopped by an automatic timer, which cuts off the fuel supply after the appropriate number of seconds.

This kind of contest is called duration flying and the very best models can glide for at least three minutes after a very short engine run. Many models are fitted with a de-thermalizing tailplane that pops-up after a set time. This makes the model come back to earth quickly.

The tubular fuselage is made from balsa wood or fibre glass. The wings and tailplane can be sheet balsa or traditional tissue-covered framework.

Pylon

Long thin fuselage

In order to glide well, the model needs to climb as high as it can during the short power run. This means having a powerful racing engine which will take the plane up as far as possible, very quickly.

A timer cuts off the engine after ten seconds, and can also control the automatic rudder and pop-up de-thermaliser tail, if they are fitted (see page 11). Like all free-flight models competition planes are trimmed to circle to stop them being lost.

Fin

Tailplane has small fins

Pilot wears ear protectors as the engine is very noisy.

Flapper wings

Rubber band

Plunger

Plunger holds the trailing edge up. Wing is thin and flat bottomed.

Trailing edge

Plunger released. Rubber band pulls down trailing edge and wing becomes curved for glide.

▲A competition model has to do two things, climb very fast and glide for as long as possible. These two actions are quite different and best carried out by wings of a different shape. Thin flat-bottomed wings are best for the steep climb, but a more curved wing gives the lift necessary for a good glide. Some models are fitted with a wing which changes shape when the engine stops. They are called "flappers" or Variable Geometry models.

17

POWERED FREE-FLIGHT

There are two main types of free-flight power models—sports models, which are made for the fun of building and flying, and competition models built to international contest regulations and designed to win competitions.

It is easy to lose a free-flight model of any kind, as they can fly out of sight quickly. To prevent this happening, trim your model to fly in a circle. Fly in a large field away from trees, houses and overhead wires, when there is little wind. Keep flights quite short at first.

Engines

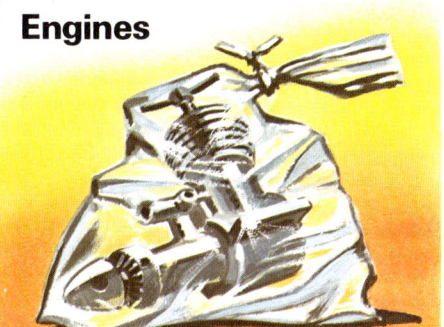

▲The engine is the most expensive part of a powered model so look after it well. Clean your engine after every flight and store it in a plastic bag when it is not in use. A dirty engine is never efficient.

Once you have one engine you can use it in several different models. The size of engine that a sports model needs is determined by the model's weight and wingspan. Most kits and plans suggest a suitable size range. It is better to make a light model and fit the smaller engine.

It can be difficult to compare diesel and glowplug engines as they are often measured in different units. Glowplugs are often measured in cubic inches (cu in) and diesels in cubic centimetres (cc). The most popular international competition class uses a 2.5cc (0.15cu in) engine. Competition engines are powerful and highly tuned.

Sports models

Sports models are usually designed with a high wing, tilted up at an ample dihedral angle. This helps to produce stable flights. The engine run is kept short by limiting the amount of fuel in the tank. You can fit a special tank made from clear plastic, with graduations marked on the side. After a few runs you will be able to tell how long a certain quantity of fuel will power the engine.

High wing with a big dihedral angle to give lift and stable flight.

Small 1cc diesel engines provide enough power for this kind of model.

This transparent free-flight fuel tank is very small and shows the quantity of fuel. This means that engine runs can be timed by limiting the amount of fuel used.

Model is travelling at about 25kph (15mph), as it takes off.

Many sports models are fitted with wheels and can take off from the ground, as long as it is a firm, flat surface like short grass, tarmac or concrete.

CO_2 engine

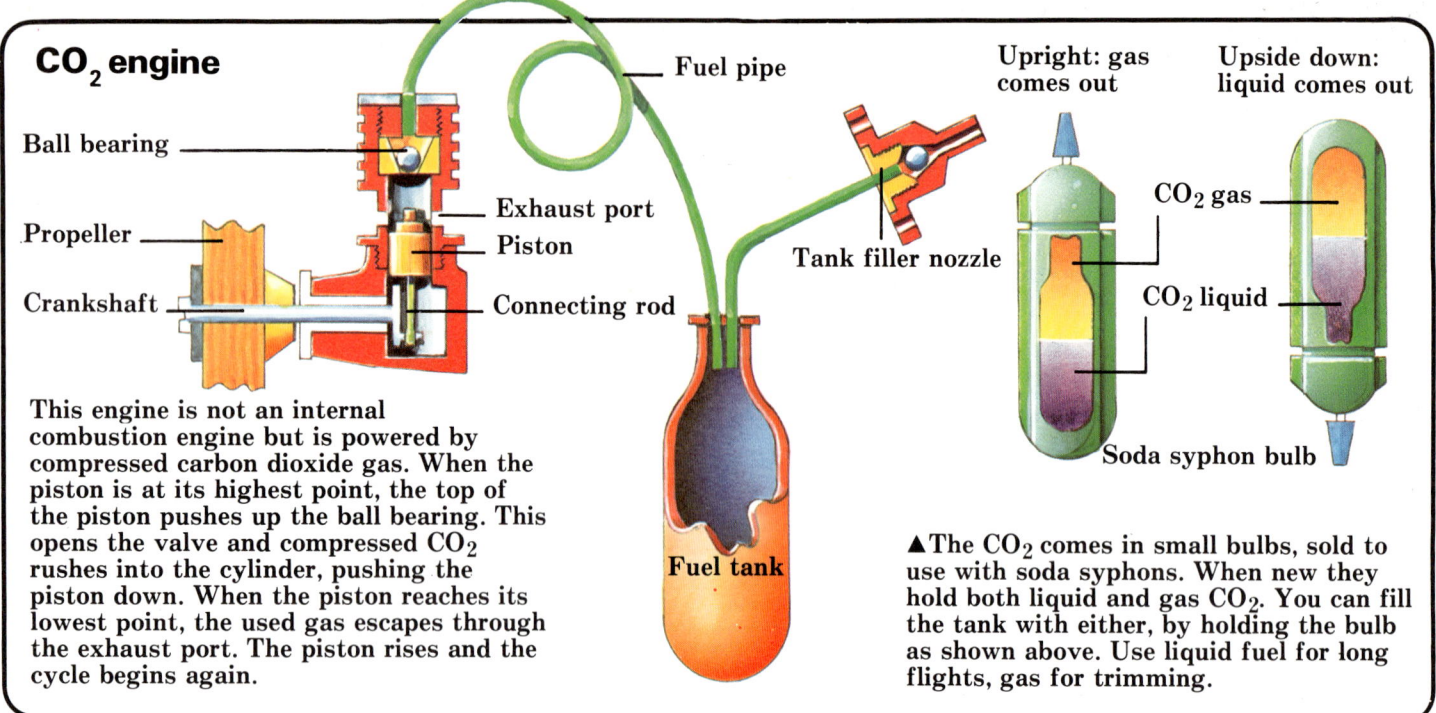

This engine is not an internal combustion engine but is powered by compressed carbon dioxide gas. When the piston is at its highest point, the top of the piston pushes up the ball bearing. This opens the valve and compressed CO_2 rushes into the cylinder, pushing the piston down. When the piston reaches its lowest point, the used gas escapes through the exhaust port. The piston rises and the cycle begins again.

▲The CO_2 comes in small bulbs, sold to use with soda syphons. When new they hold both liquid and gas CO_2. You can fill the tank with either, by holding the bulb as shown above. Use liquid fuel for long flights, gas for trimming.

Test bench

Always test an engine before your first flight, even if it is second-hand. This will give you a chance to see how it performs and to become familiar with it. New engines often need to be "run-in", like a new car, before they work efficiently. About 10 to 20 tanks of fuel should be enough to run-in most engines.

Testing and running-in should be done on a test bench (use any old table or chair as a bench). Mount your engine securely on a piece of hardwood, as explained in the following pictures, and fix it firmly to the bench. Never run engines in the house as they are very noisy and dirty. Always treat engines and fuel with care – they can be dangerous.

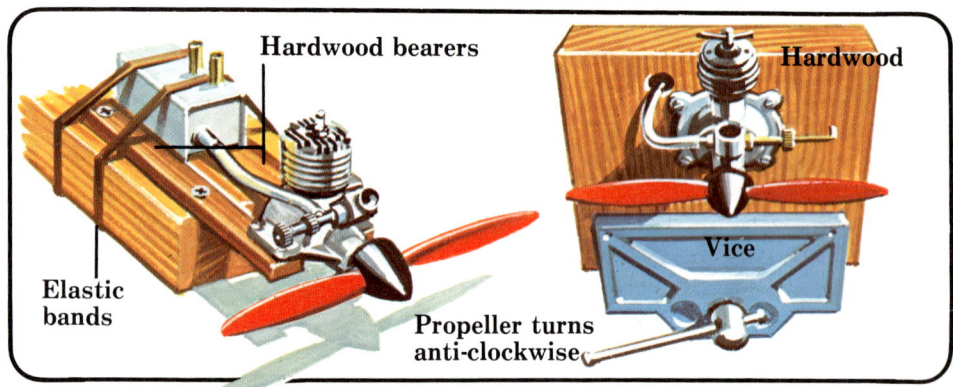

▲This picture shows how to mount a beam-mounted engine for testing. Fix the engine to two hardwood bearers and then screw the bearers to a block of wood. Secure the block of wood to the test bench.

▲This is a radially mounted engine. It should be screwed to a piece of hardwood held securely in a vice, fixed to the test bench. Engines run anti-clockwise when viewed from the front.

Starting-up

Most manufacturers supply some instructions explaining how to start their engines. You may find starting an engine very difficult, however, unless you have help from someone who has done it before. CO_2 engines are the easiest sort to start but they are best for small lightweight planes.

After filling the fuel tank of a glowplug or diesel engine, turn the needle valve to the recommended setting. Cover the air intake and turn the propeller over about four times. This draws fuel into the engine from the tank and is called choking. Some engines need to have a few drops of fuel put through the exhaust port instead, this is called priming. Make sure you use the right fuel.

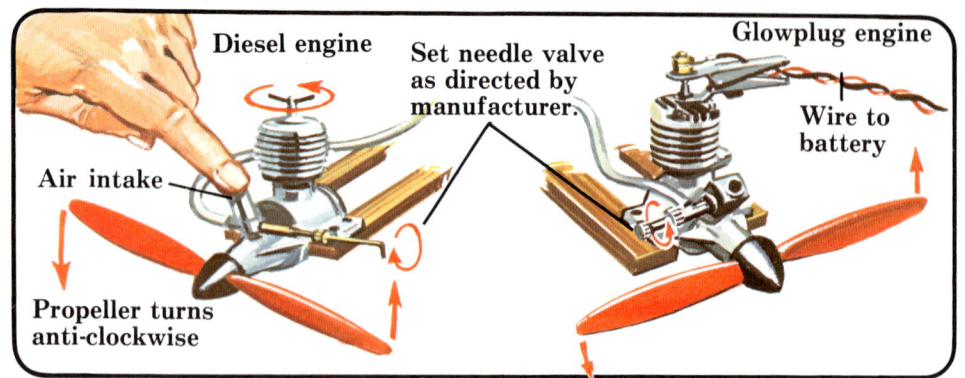

▲This picture shows how to choke a diesel engine. When you have done this, wear thick gloves and flick the left blade of the propeller down hard to start the engine. Pull your hand away very fast as a propeller can hurt you when it is spinning.

▲When a glowplug engine is primed or choked, clip on the battery clip as shown here. This heats the glowplug which should start the engine when you flick the propeller sharply. Disconnect the battery once the engine is running properly.

15

Making microfilm

Microfilm is made from a mixture of dope, amyl acetate and castor oil. It cannot be bought ready made so modellers have to make their own. This is done by dropping some of the mixture onto a surface of water in a sink or bath. It forms a very thin film which can be gently lifted off with a wire loop or balsa frame and then applied to the model.

Microfilm models are the most delicate type of flying model. They are made from the very thinnest, lightest strips of balsa wood and covered with an ultra-thin chemical film, called microfilm. These models are so fragile that they can be blown to bits by a sneeze or someone walking past during a flight.

World championship models weigh only one gramme and fly very, very slowly, at a speed even less than the slowest walk. They are usually flown in gigantic airship hangars, or even in large caves, where the air is still and the models have plenty of room. The very best models can remain in the air for over 40 minutes.

Round-the-pole flying

Round-the-pole flying is another branch of indoor modelling that can take place in a normal large room or hall and is easy enough for a beginner. It is a little like control-line flying, as the models fly in circles on two lines. In this case the pilot stands outside the flying circle and the models fly round a pole.

The models are powered by an electric motor. Power is carried to the motor along the fine copper flying lines from a battery. The picture below shows how this system works.

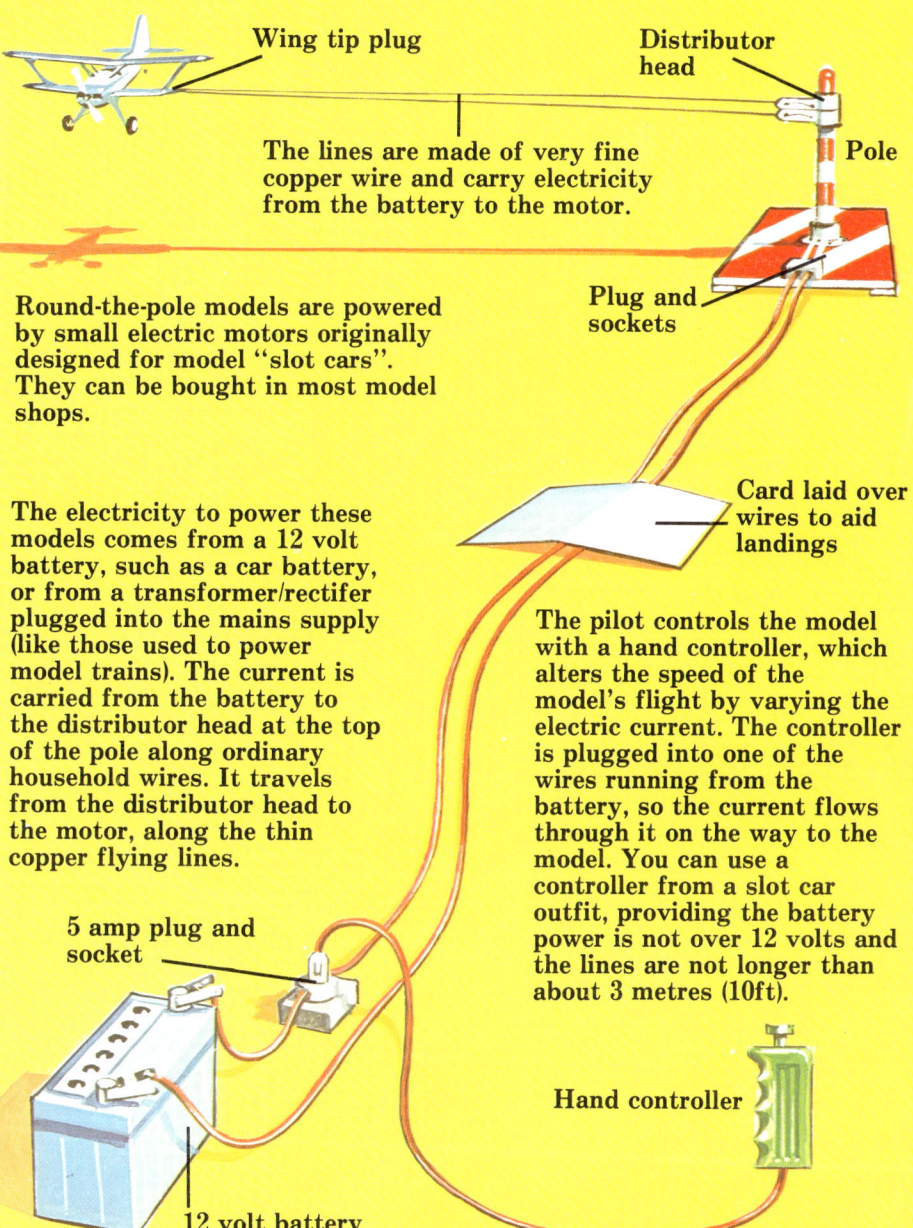

Round-the-pole models are powered by small electric motors originally designed for model "slot cars". They can be bought in most model shops.

The electricity to power these models comes from a 12 volt battery, such as a car battery, or from a transformer/rectifer plugged into the mains supply (like those used to power model trains). The current is carried from the battery to the distributor head at the top of the pole along ordinary household wires. It travels from the distributor head to the motor, along the thin copper flying lines.

The pilot controls the model with a hand controller, which alters the speed of the model's flight by varying the electric current. The controller is plugged into one of the wires running from the battery, so the current flows through it on the way to the model. You can use a controller from a slot car outfit, providing the battery power is not over 12 volts and the lines are not longer than about 3 metres (10ft).

Many kinds of model are suitable for converting to flying round the pole. Lots of people fly scale models round the pole. It is also possible to make a model perform stunts or to fly several at once in races or combat. Models can range in size from a wingspan of 30cm to up to 100cm (1ft-3ft).

The line length can also vary a great deal from 1.5m to 15m (5ft-50ft). However it is best to stick to lines of about 3m (10ft) or less if you are using a 12 volt battery.

Longer lines need more power and this can cause overheating in the hand controller.

RADIO-CONTROL

Only radio-control equipment can give you complete control over all aspects of a model aircraft's flight. With the sophisticated systems which are available today, you can fly a model in any direction, vary its speed and height, take part in races and perform aerobatic stunts. The only real disadvantage to radio-control is the price. It can be extremely expensive.

Like other advanced skills, flying radio-controlled models is something which you have to learn and practise if you want to do it well.

Learning to fly

▲The easiest way to learn how to fly a radio-controlled model is with the help of an experienced pilot and a "buddy-box". This is a dual control system, pictured above, where the model is flown up to a safe height by the experienced pilot and then taken over by the learner. Both pilots have their own controls but the instructor can take over if the learner pilot is having problems with the flight.

The best sort of model to fly while learning to pilot with radio-control equipment is a trainer plane. They are designed to be stable in the air and easy to fly.

Transmitting

▼The picture below shows a radio-control transmitter. This sends out instructions to the model in the form of coded radio signals. The signals are picked up by a receiver inside the plane, de-coded and carried out.

The pilot transmits the coded signal by moving the control sticks as shown below. The engine control is "dead"—it stays in the position it is pushed to. The other controls have to be held in place. All controls are "proportional", which means the further they are pushed the stronger the response of the plane.

This is a four channel system which controls four parts of the plane; the engine, ailerons, elevators and rudder. Some systems have up to six channels and can control other parts as well as those shown here.

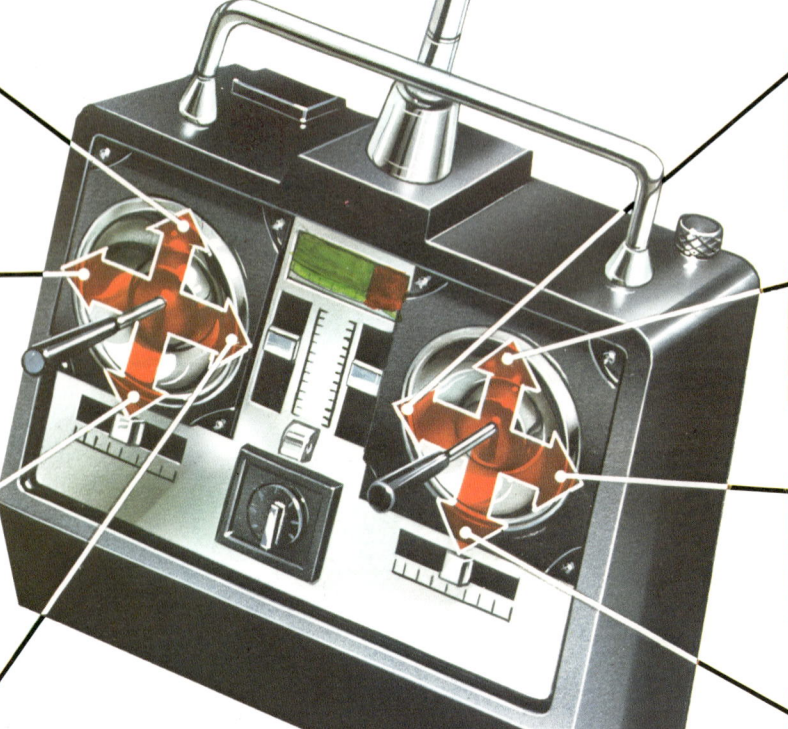

Increase engine speed — Engine speeds up

Left rudder — Plane turns to the left

Decrease engine speed — Engine slows down

Right rudder — Plane turns to the right

Left aileron — Plane dips to the left

Down elevator — Plane begins to dive

Right aileron — Plane dips to the right

Up elevator — Plane begins to climb

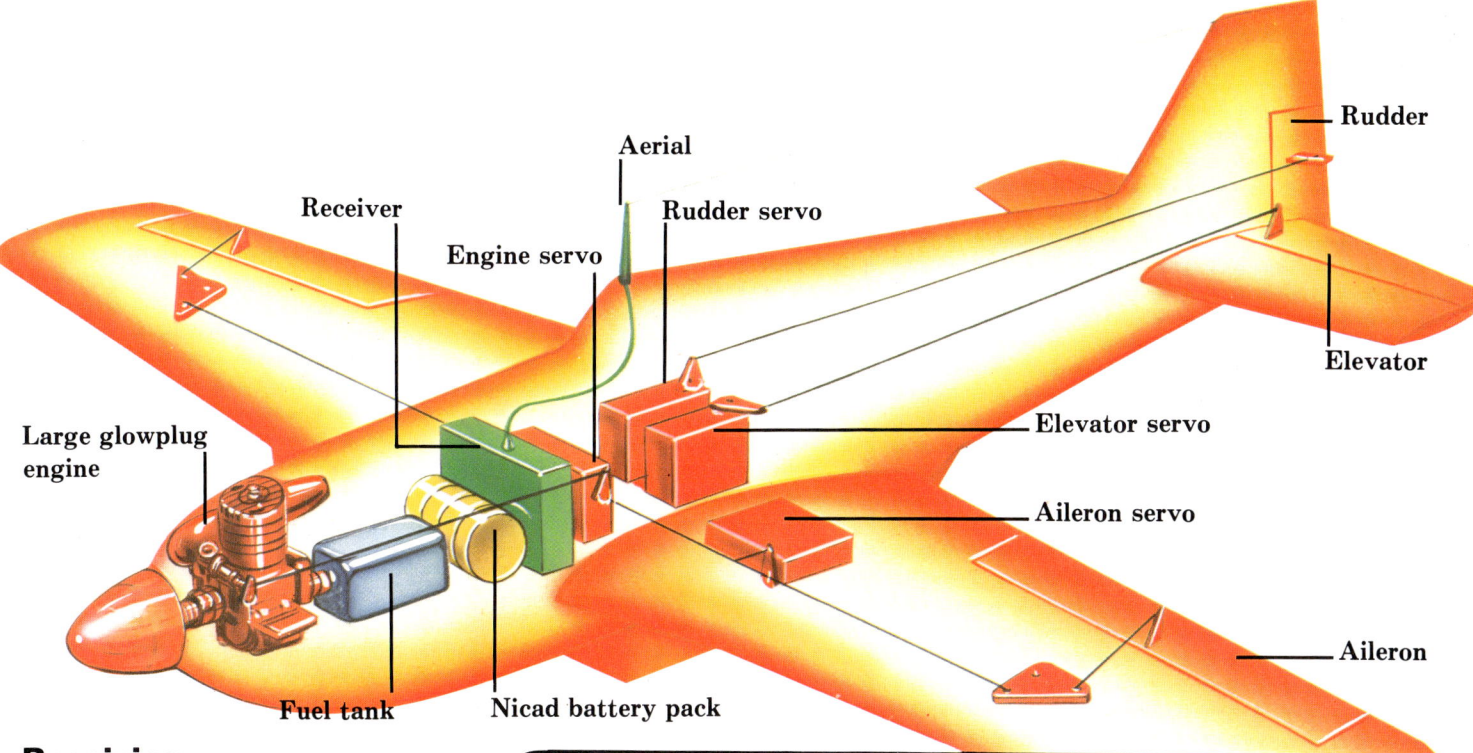

Receiving

▲The picture above shows the radio-control equipment that has to be fitted inside a model flown on a four channel system.

The receiver picks up the radio signal, de-codes it and passes the instructions to the "servos". The servos have tiny motors and move the part of the plane they control in accordance with the instructions from the receiver. There is one servo for each channel and this controls one part of the plane.

As this is a radio-controlled powered model it needs not only an engine and a fuel tank, but also a battery pack to power the receiver and the four servos.

Colour codes

Grey/Brown	Orange/Yellow
Brown	Yellow
Brown/Red	Yellow/Green
Red	Green
Red/Orange	Green/Blue
Orange	Blue

▲Radio-control equipment must be tuned to an exact radio frequency, known as a "spot frequency". There are 12 spot frequencies and each one is represented by a single colour or a pair of colours. These colours are shown above.

Pilots put a bright coloured pennant on their transmitter's aerial to show which spot they are using. If two pilots were to fly on the same frequency, their signals would get mixed up and they would lose control of their models.

Radio-controlled gliding

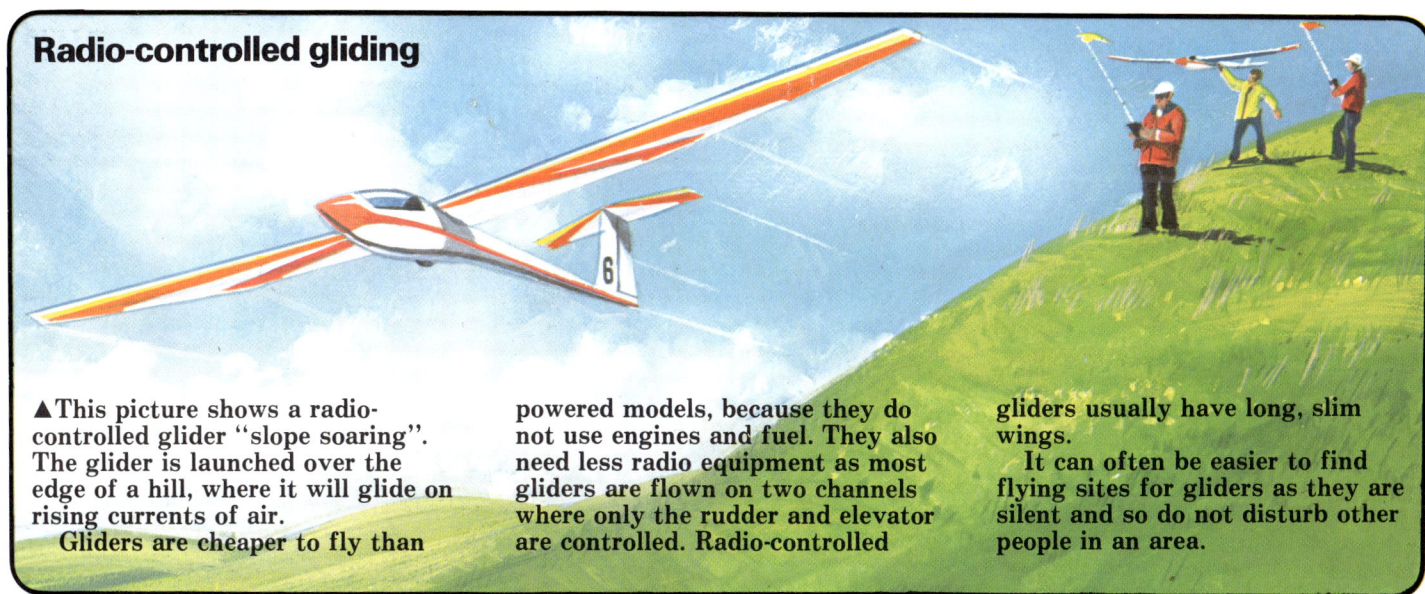

▲This picture shows a radio-controlled glider "slope soaring". The glider is launched over the edge of a hill, where it will glide on rising currents of air.

Gliders are cheaper to fly than powered models, because they do not use engines and fuel. They also need less radio equipment as most gliders are flown on two channels where only the rudder and elevator are controlled. Radio-controlled gliders usually have long, slim wings.

It can often be easier to find flying sites for gliders as they are silent and so do not disturb other people in an area.

AEROBATICS AND RACING

Speed racing and aerobatic stunting are probably the most skilled and exciting aspects of model aircraft flying. They can only be performed by radio-controlled or control-line planes as the pilot must have complete control over the model's flight.

This sort of flying is very difficult, even for expert pilots. It takes a great deal of concentration to race a model at speeds of 150kph (95mph) or to pilot it through the stunt manoeuvres pictured on these pages.

Control-line stunts

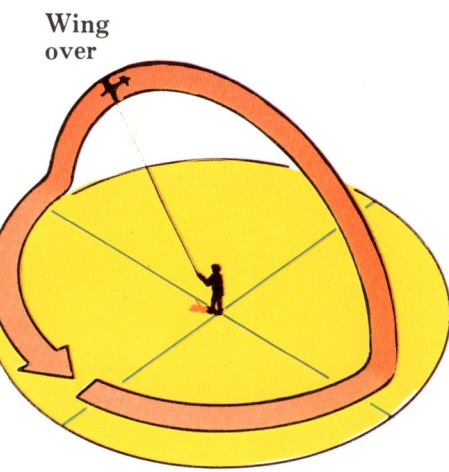
Wing over

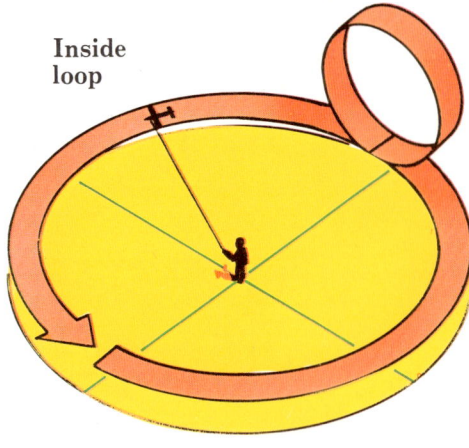
Inside loop

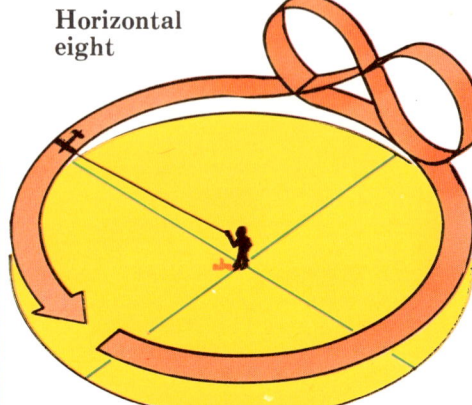
Horizontal eight

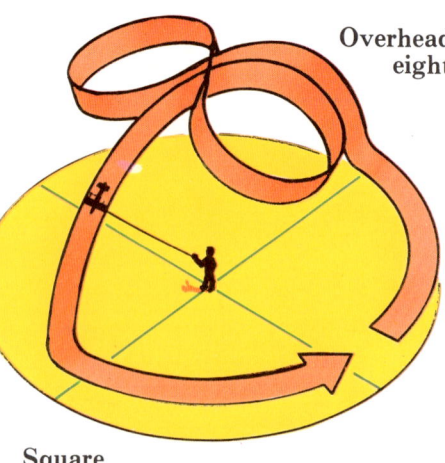
Overhead eight

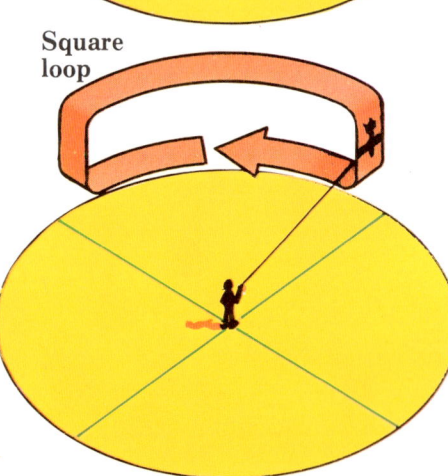
Square loop

Control-line team racing

▼These three pilots are competing in a control-line team race. It is called team racing because each pilot has a partner, the pit mechanic, who re-fuels the model during the race. The planes fly heats of 100 laps, often in less than four minutes and reach speeds of over 140kph (90mph).

According to the competition rules the planes must be realistic semi-scale models.

This type of model must also be sturdy and well constructed as team racing can be very rough.

The pit mechanics wear crash helmets to protect their heads from the models and the lines.

Pit mechanic

Pressurized fuel can

▶The pit mechanic has to grab the model as it touches-down, making sure he does not get in the way of the other pilots, models and lines. He has a can of pressurized fuel strapped to his arm and can re-fuel, re-start and re-launch the plane in a matter of seconds.

Publicity models

▲Thousands of model airliners, like the one shown here, are made for airline companies and aircraft manufacturers. You can see them in advertising displays at airline and travel agent's offices. They are usually made from solid plastic and some have a cut-away section that shows the inside of the plane. This kind of model can look like a real plane if photographed against a suitable background. They often appear on poster and magazine advertisements.

difficult kind of effect to achieve using models is the sort of formation flying seen here.

Models used in films are often very big – up to one quarter of the size of the real plane. They are made by professional model makers who usually also pilot them during the filming. Models are particularly useful for films about the past as vintage aircraft are rare and too valuable to blow-up.

PLANE WORDS

When you begin aeromodelling you will read and hear lots of words which you may not have come across before. This page explains some of the most common terms which are used to describe both full-size and model aircraft.

Number of wings

▲Monoplane – a plane with one set of wings.

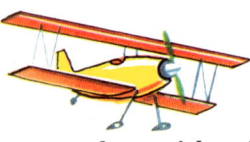

▲Biplane – a plane with a double set of wings.

▲Triplane – a plane with a triple set of wings.

Wing position

▲Low wing – this type of wing is most suitable on control-line or radio-control planes as it tends to be unstable.

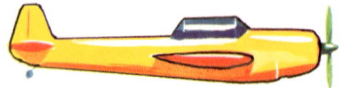

▲Mid wing – this is a more stable design, but is rarely used on free-flight models.

▲High wing – a very stable design, that is widely used for training and sports free-flight models.

▲Shoulder wing – held above the fuselage on a pylon. This is a stable design used on powered free-flight competition models.

Angle of wings

Having wings tilted up at a dihedral angle makes a plane's flight more stable. This is important to free-flight models which are not controlled by a pilot. A pilot can correct the effects of wind on a plane, but an unpiloted model has to rely on its design and trimming to keep stable.

▲Simple dihedral – often used for powered sports models.

▲Tip dihedral – centre section of the wing is flat but the wing tips are turned up. This is the usual design for gliders.

▲Polydihedral – this is a combination of simple dihedral and tip dihedral. It is often used for competition power models.

Wing shapes

The size and shape of a model's wings will affect the way in which it flies. So different kinds of models have different wings which produce the appropriate flight.

▲High aspect ratio – this long thin wing is common on many types of gliders.

▲Low aspect ratio – a short fat wing used for sports and trainer models as it is very strong.

▲Swept back – this sort of wing shape is usually used on high speed planes such as racers.

▲Delta – this type of design does not have a tailplane and so is a type of flying wing.

Aerofoils

Aerofoil (or airfoil) is the word which describes the shape of a wing in cross-section. There are many different designs each with its own advantages. Some designs make flight fast under power, others produce lots of lift. So aerofoil shapes vary from model to model, according to the way they are meant to fly.

▲Flat bottomed – often used on free-flight models as it creates good lift and climbs well.

▲Undercambered – this design produces most lift but is not suitable for high speed. Most common on gliders and rubber-powered models.

▲Symmetrical – as both the top and bottom of this wing are the same, it is good for aerobatic control-line and radio-controlled models which spend a lot of time flying upside-down.

▲Speed – this wing is thin and streamlined to reduce drag as it flies through the air. Used on many types of speed and racing models.

Tail types

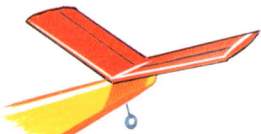

▲V tail – tailplane is not flat but made into a "V" shape. This kind of tailplane does not need a fin.

▲T tail – flat tailplane raised above the fuselage out of the disturbed air created by an engine or wings.

Flying sites

Finding somewhere to fly model aircraft can be very difficult, especially if you live in a town.

Chuck gliders are probably the most convenient sort of model as they can be flown on a site about the size of a football pitch.

Control-line models need a similar amount of space but their engines make a lot of noise.

Powered free-flight planes also make a great deal of noise and need a site up to four times as big as a football pitch.

▼If you are in the countryside take care not to disturb wildlife, crops and farm animals.

Never fly close to electricity power lines, houses or trees as this can be dangerous.

Disused airports, and large sports fields can be ideal flying sites. Always get permission to use land before you fly. If you have an engine-powered plane try to use a silencer as this cuts down the noise level.

GOING FURTHER

Club news

Once you have successfully built and flown a few simple aircraft models, you will be skilled enough to make more difficult models. At this stage it is a good idea to join your local aeromodelling club. You can learn a great deal simply by being with other modellers, looking at the models they have made and watching them fly.

Clubs often have permission to use good flying sites and sometimes organize competitions and outings to modelling events. Your local model shop will probably be able to put you in touch with the nearest club.

Most countries have a national body which controls and organizes modelling competitions and events.

GREAT BRITAIN: the S.M.A.E. (Society of Model Aeronautical Engineers).

U.S.A.: the A.M.A. (Academy of Model Aeronautics).

CANADA: the M.A.A.C. (Model Aeronautics Association of Canada).

AUSTRALIA: the M.A.A.A. (Model Airplane Association of Australia).

NEW ZEALAND: the N.Z.M.A.A. (New Zealand Model Aeronautical Association Inc).

These organizations and many other national associations are affiliated to an international governing body, the F.A.I. (Fédération Aéronautique Internationale).

The F.A.I. set all the regulations for contests and their officials supervise international model competitions.

Further reading

A collection of books and magazines about aircraft modelling can be very useful. Look at books carefully before buying, as they are often very technical and meant for expert modellers. Your local library may have a range of books which you can borrow.

Magazines often have articles aimed at beginners which explain how to make and fly different types of model aircraft. They also publish information about competitions, new products and have lots of advertisements which will help you to choose the equipment you need.

Books to read

All About Model Aircraft. Peter Chinn. (Argus Books)

The Model Aircraft Handbook. Howard G. McEntee. (Hale)

The World of Model Aircraft. Guy R. Williams. (Andre Deutch)

Model Aircraft. Martin Hedges. (Hamlyn/Bison)

How to Design And Build Flying Models. Keith Laumer. (Hale)

The Encyclopedia of Model Aircraft. Vic Smeed. (Octopus)

Magazines to read. Most are published once a month.

GREAT BRITAIN: Aeromodeller, Radio Modeller, Radio Control Models & Electronics. Model Maker

U.S.A.: Flying Models, Model Aviation, Radio Control Modeler.

AUSTRALIA: Airborne.

NEW ZEALAND: N.Z.M.A.A. produces a Newsletter.

PRINTED IN BELGIUM BY
proost
INTERNATIONAL BOOK PRODUCTION

INDOOR FLYING

These pages show the three kinds of models designed to be flown indoors: microfilm covered models, paper covered models and round-the-pole models. Microfilm and paper covered models are both rubber-powered and fly very slowly. Round-the-pole planes have small electric motors.

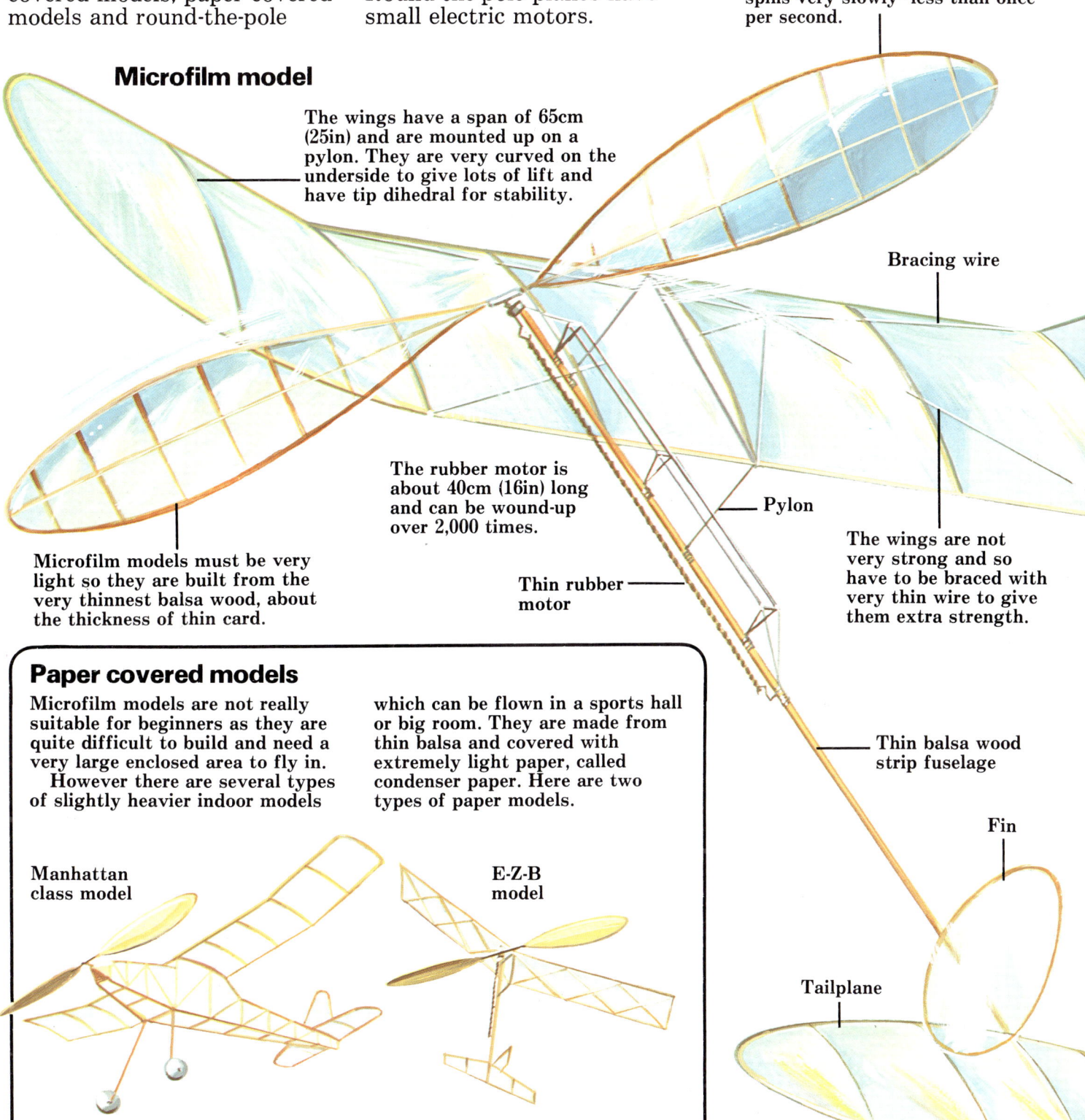

Microfilm model

The wings have a span of 65cm (25in) and are mounted up on a pylon. They are very curved on the underside to give lots of lift and have tip dihedral for stability.

Microfilm models must be very light so they are built from the very thinnest balsa wood, about the thickness of thin card.

The rubber motor is about 40cm (16in) long and can be wound-up over 2,000 times.

Thin rubber motor

The propeller is also made from very light balsa and microfilm. It spins very slowly—less than once per second.

Bracing wire

Pylon

The wings are not very strong and so have to be braced with very thin wire to give them extra strength.

Thin balsa wood strip fuselage

Fin

Tailplane

Paper covered models

Microfilm models are not really suitable for beginners as they are quite difficult to build and need a very large enclosed area to fly in.

However there are several types of slightly heavier indoor models which can be flown in a sports hall or big room. They are made from thin balsa and covered with extremely light paper, called condenser paper. Here are two types of paper models.

Manhattan class model

E-Z-B model

▲Manhattan class models have a quite conventional design and must weigh six grammes. They can fly for up to 10 minutes.

▲E-Z-B (easy bee) models are similar to microfilm models in design, but are less fragile and easier to fly and build.

Learning to fly

▲Control-line models need two people to launch them, the pilot who controls from the handle and a helper, who releases the plane into the air. Before launching, make sure that there are no knots in the lines and that they are firmly attached to the handle and the model. Check that the controls move freely, in the right direction and that the pilot is holding the handle the right way up, with the down line at the bottom.

Unlike other model planes, control-line aircraft should be launched in the same direction as the wind is blowing towards. The engine makes a lot of noise so use a pre-arranged hand signal to show your helper when to launch the plane. If the model has an undercarriage it can take off from the ground.

▲The model flies round you in a circle and, as you have to turn with it, you may feel dizzy. Fixing your eyes on the model will help to combat this. Keep flights short at first, about four or five laps at a time.

▲Control-line models respond very quickly to movements of the control handle. Most beginners apply too much up or down movement, too suddenly. This is called "over-control" and often results in the model crashing.

▲While you are learning to fly on control-lines move the handle by lifting the whole of your arm rather than by moving just your wrist. Try to keep the plane on a level flight path at a height of about two metres (6ft).

Control-line combat

This picture shows two control-line models taking part in a combat competition. Each plane has a long streamer attached to its tailplane, which the other plane attacks with its propeller. These contests last for five minutes and the winner is the pilot who makes the most cuts in the opposing streamer.

Combat flying is very difficult but exciting and great fun to watch. The planes swoop and climb, flying in spectacular manoeuvres as they chase each other, trying to avoid the opposing propeller, yet also attempting to cut the other's streamer.

These models are specially built to be very lightweight.